20°

40°

40°

40°

JAN. 30, 1850

FEB. 4, 1850

RIO DE JANIEPO
JAN 10~12, 1850

60°

FEB. 22, 1850

WILDREBUSH
MR. 4,
APR. 3, 1850

80°

BOB
BLAKE

MAR. II, 1850

100°

APRIL 26, 1850

120°

20°

40°

Date Due

EUREKA

EUREKA

FROM

CLEVELAND

BY *SHIP*

TO

CALIFORNIA

1849-1850

Robert Samuel Fletcher

DUKE UNIVERSITY PRESS   Durham, N. C. 1959

The Library of Congress has cataloged this book as follows:

Fletcher, Robert Samuel, 1900–
　　Eureka, from Cleveland by ship to California, 1849-1850.
　　Durham, N. C., Duke University Press, 1959.

　　145 p.　illus.　21 cm.

　　1. Eureka (Barque)　2. Voyages to the Pacific coast.　3. Ohio—
Hist.—1787-1865.

F865.F62　　　　　　　　917.94　　　　　　　59–9865 ‡

Library of Congress

PRINTED IN THE UNITED STATES OF AMERICA
BY THE SEEMAN PRINTERY, INC., DURHAM, N. C.

Of course,
this is for Dan.

The publication of this book
was assisted by a grant to the
Duke University Press by the
Ford Foundation.

Acknowledgments

MY FIRST INDEBTEDNESS is to the late Nora Abbe
of Elyria, who entertained my wife and me when
we transcribed the journal of her grandfather,
Eleazer Abbe. I read off the journal as my wife,
Mary Elizabeth Abbey Fletcher, wrote it down on
Oberlin College blue books. Miss Abbe commented on the transcription, and then served the
tea and cookies as we discussed the adventures of
the Elyria farmer and teamster who was her grandfather and diarist of the voyage of the *Eureka* to
California in 1849-1850.

Those who have done any historical research
know to what extent it is the librarians who actually perform the foundation work. In my work
on the story of the *Eureka* this is more than ordi-
narily true. Mrs. Alene L. White, librarian of the
Western Reserve Historical Society of Cleveland,
contributed of her time and information in the
early stages of the work in a very large way. A
very considerable part of the letters printed in the
Cleveland papers were found in files in the Western Reserve Historical Society, as was the MS

letter from Cyrus Bassett written to G. G. Washburn from California.

California librarians have been extremely helpful in this research carried on from Ohio and New York State. I am especially indebted to Mrs. Helen Harding Bretnor of the Bancroft Library of the General Library of the University of California at Berkeley; Miss Jeanette M. Hitchcock of the Stanford University Libraries of Stanford, California; Miss Mabel R. Gillis, Miss Caroline Wenzel, and Miss Helen M. Bruner of the California State Library of Sacramento and San Francisco; Miss Haydée Noya of the Department of Manuscripts of the Henry E. Huntington Library of San Marino; and Mrs. Rogers Paratt, director of the California Historical Society. The author is also indebted to Miss Phyllis Pope of the James Prendergast Free Library of Jamestown, New York; Miss Alice J. Pickup of the Buffalo Historical Society; Miss Maude Lamley of the Milan (Ohio) Public Library; Mrs. Elleine H. Stones of the Burton Historical Collection at the Detroit Public Library; Mr. E. Charles D. Marriage, librarian of the Nevada State Library at Carson City, Nevada; and Miss Esther Usher, assistant librarian of the Essex Institute of Salem, Massachusetts. Mr. Clarence S. Metcalf, librarian of the Cleveland Public Library, and Miss Florence M. Gifford, head of the General Reference Division of the Cleveland Public Library, took an interest in the *Eureka* before I did. Jewell R. Dean told the story from newspaper accounts collected under the direction of Mr. Metcalf in an article in the *Plain Dealer* (Feb. 27, 1944), and Miss Gifford somewhat expanded this account in an article in the *Inland Seas* in the summer of 1957 (XIII, 105-109). Those who gave valuable assistance to the author included Mrs. Helen B. Mathews of Painesville; James F. Abel of Winnemuca, Nevada; William Galbraith Smith of Washington, D. C., who lent the daguerreotype of Llewellyn App Rogers; Mrs. Helen S. Griffin, secretary and librarian of the Society of California Pioneers; Mr. Claybourne D. Sampson of Jamestown, N. Y.; Mrs. Leon Johnson of Warren, Pennsylvania; Theresa Gay of Oakland, California, who put me in touch with the late Warren T. Russell; Mr. Marcus W. Price, Director of the General Records Division of the National Archives, who made available to me the consul's report of the arrival of the *Eureka* in Acapulco; and H. E. Johnson, editor of the Painesville *Telegraph,* who helped me get in touch with surviving relatives of Colbert Huntington. Wallace B. Johnson of Hamilton College furnished to me biographical data on Llewellyn App Rogers; Mr. Lucius Rogers Shero of Swarthmore, Pa., sent me the address of William Galbraith Smith, the present owner of the daguerreotype; Mrs. Robert W. Mackay was also helpful in following up Rogers, as was also David Potter. William Kaye Lamb, Dominion Archivist of Canada, provided me with a pertinent item from the Quebec *Ga-*

zette. John O. Bowman went to some trouble to secure a photostat of a notice from the Jamestown *Journal.* Mr. Ralph McCombs of Columbus, Ohio, lent me the diary of Olive Brown.

I am glad to acknowledge the obligation which anyone inevitably incurs to the reference librarians when working in Oberlin, to Miss Mary Venn, to Miss Leila Holloway and to Mr. Jack Saeger. My association with the Lorain County Historical Society first brought the *Eureka* to my attention, and the Eleazer Abbe journal as well.

Oberlin, Ohio

Robert Samuel Fletcher

Editorial Note: Throughout I have eschewed the intrusive editorial [*sic*], feeling not only that it would destroy the reader's pleasure in some highly original orthography, but that such knuckle-rapping would also be a "vary unjentelmanly" way to treat those who provided the data upon which this narrative was based.

R. S. F.

Contents

Illustrations

EUREKA

1.

A Name

OVER a hundred years ago a party of gold hunters sailed from Cleveland through the Welland Canal, through the St. Lawrence and its canals to Quebec and out to sea, past the Cape Verde Islands, to Rio de Janeiro, south and around Cape Horn, north to Valparaiso, and then to California and San Francisco, even though it took nine months . . . . The first necessity for such a voyage was obviously a ship.

Fortunately the southern shore of Lake Erie was shipbuilding country. In the first half of the nineteenth century many vessels floated out from the short rivers which flow into the lake from the south: the Ashtabula, the Grand, the Cuyahoga, the Black, the Vermilion, and the Huron. White pine floated down from the upper lakes and oak hauled in by sled during the snowy winters by the local farmers provided the timber.

By mid-century a swarm of shallow-draft, top-heavy water monsters, with churning paddle wheels and slim, twin stacks bannered with smoke and sparks, was parading the channels of the Ohio and Mississippi, but most of the commerce of the Great Lakes was still windborne. Sailing ships never had a chance along the cramped, meandering courses of the muddy rivers, but on the blue-green expanse of the lakes there was room to tack or to roll along freely and relatively safely before a stiff breeze or even a gale.

True, the *Walk-in-the-Water* had visited Dunkirk, Erie, Cleveland, Sandusky, and Detroit as early as 1818, and most of the passenger traffic had been taken over before 1850 by steamboats, but until after the Civil War a great deal of the pork, grain, lumber, and heavier products of the eastern factories bound for the West was carried in sloops, schooners, brigs, or barques, whose sails were always in sight from the Ohio shore.

Many keels were laid on the banks of the Black River in Lorain County. Great ribs were carved with saw and axe from well-seasoned oak and set perpendicular to the keels, until the drafty wooden skeletons stood high above the surrounding sheds and warehouses. Then four-inch planks were spiked on and finished with adze and plane, and the pine decks were laid. For weeks before the launching the calkers' mallets rang, as oakum was packed into the seams of hull and deck. After the launching the pine masts were stepped, and riggers raised the spars and booms and spliced and lashed the stays and shrouds. Then the sails were bent to the yards, and she was ready to go.[1]

Some schooners built here were lost within the year, perhaps during some wild November storm; a barque from the same skids may have served for thirty years and never left Lake Erie. But here was launched a brig, which, rerigged as a barque, tasted the salt of two great oceans and, at last report, lay abandoned in a near-forgotten harbor on the southwest coast of Mexico.

Probably no one will ever know what premonition led her builders to christen her *Eureka*.

[1] On building a ship in the lakes, see H. C. Inches, "Wooden Ship Building," *Inland Seas*, VII (Spring, 1951), 3-12.

```
                  2.

        Black River
        Backgrounds
```

He who goes on a journey must start from some-
where.   Adventurers leave behind them the town
where "nothing ever happens."   This is one justi-
fication for their going.

"Nothing ever happened" in Elyria.   It was the
only considerable town on the sixty-mile stretch of
the great stage road between Cleveland and Nor-
walk at the west; its location had been determined
by the forks and the falls of the Black River.
There three dusty, rumbling gristmills perched on
the gorge rim at the East and West falls.   Above
and south of them, between the embracing arms

of the east and west branches of the river, the neat, Greek-temple courthouse on the green marked the seat of Lorain County.[1]

Occasionally something did happen. One January day in 1847 Eleazer Abbe, a thrifty, industrious farmer and teamster, disturbed the boys playing mumblety-peg in order that he might climb the steps before the columned portico and enter the office of the county recorder. This morning he had added eighty acres to the family farm, and the deed must be registered. The official opened the paper, cracked the ledger, and pressed it flat. He made a neat entry, checked the names and date, then folded the deed again and wrote his own name on the outside across the end: "Cyrus E. Bassett, Recorder."[2]

Abbe tucked the precious document in an inner pocket, ambled out into the winter sunshine, climbed into his farm wagon, and rode slowly away down Broad Street, back to his wife and five children. Perhaps he stopped at Milo Bennett's blacksmith shop to get a horse shod, but he bumped past the Mansion House and other establishments dispensing spirituous beverages with total indifference; Eleazer Abbe was steady and dependable, a good provider. He'd never set the world on fire,

[1] Henry Howe, *Historical Collections of Ohio* (Cincinnati, 1849), pp. 314-315.
[2] The deed was in the possession of the late Miss Nora Abbe of Elyria, a granddaughter.

but Betsey Abbe didn't have to worry; he'd come home sober and taciturn as always.[3]   He was the last person you would ever expect to start out on a wild goose chase half way round the world looking for gold.

Elyria was still building, thirty years after Artemas Beebe had supervised the cutting of the first trees and the erection of the tavern and the first cabins for the proprietor, Heman Ely.   Beebe was doing fine.   Now a new Beebe hotel was rising opposite the western side of the northwest corner of the green, bigger than necessary, it seemed, for a town of only fifteen hundred people—a really imposing four-story brick structure.   The grand opening, soon after New Year's, 1848, was a "brilliant affair."   "Supper," said the Elyria *Courier,* "was furnished to 240 people, and served in a style scarcely known among us, and the music and the dancing—well dedicated was the spacious hall by the life-enjoying company, that crowded its supposed superabundant room!"   Elyria patrons had shown themselves equal to the challenge.[4] When court convened later in the month, the management entertained the entire bench and bar at another great banquet, at which toasts were

[3] On Eleazer Abbe see *Commemorative Biographical Record of the Counties of Huron and Lorain, Ohio* (Chicago, 1894), pp. 878-881; A. R. Webber, *Early History of Elyria and Her People* (Elyria, 1930), pp. 100-101; and J. G. Nichols and Cleveland Abbe, *Abbe-Abbey Genealogy* (New Haven, 1916), p. 159.
    [4] Elyria *Courier*, Jan. 4, 1848.

proposed to the "Beebe House," "The Bar," "The Judiciary," and "Bachelor Members of the Lorain Bar." These toasts must have been drunk in cold water, for the Beebe House opened as a temperance tavern.[5] The time would come when certain wanderers would look back nostalgically upon these festivities in the old home town.

Perhaps there was some connection between the temperance principles of the new hotel and the proximity of the Presbyterian Church, its spire pointed toward Heaven, on the same side of the square directly to the south. This was the church of many of the most respectable first families; this was the church of tavern-keeper Artemas Beebe and of Heman Ely, the founder of the town. The fine new edifice was dedicated not long after the opening of the tavern, on May 17, 1848. "The ladies of the town have carpeted and cushioned the whole house," reported the local paper. "Strangers pronounce the building the finest west of the Alleganies." The church has since been torn down, but surviving photographs mark it as one of the more effective examples of the religious Gothic of the time.[6]

Cyrus Bassett, who served as county recorder

[5] *Ibid.*, Feb. 1, 1848.

[6] *Ibid.*, April 18 and May 9, 1848. There is a list of members and other material in the *Dedication Souvenir—First Congregational Church* (Elyria, 1900). It became the First Congregational Church in 1879. The building erected in 1848 was torn down in 1898.

from 1843 to 1849, when he left for California, was
one of the more active workers in the various cultural and social causes which leavened the life of
the "Yankee belt" in those days. He joined Beebe
and others to ask for contributions for five million
"suffering poor in Ireland": "To America the
blessed task is given to save a generous and warm
hearted people."[7] When the Friends of Peace and
Universal Brotherhood of Lorain County met at
the courthouse on June 12, 1849, Bassett was
elected one of the secretaries, and Hamilton Hill,
of near-by Oberlin College, was named as a dele-
gate to the World's Peace Convention at Paris.[8]
Bassett was associated with G. G. Washburn, editor
of one of the local papers, as an officer of the Elyria
chapter of the Sons of Temperance, an organization which, appropriately, had rooms in the tee-
total Beebe House.[9] As secretary of the Elyria
Natural History Society, he issued announcements
of scientific lectures—Dr. Hubbard on "Nitrogen
and Atmosphere" and "Carbon and Its Com-
pounds," and Dr. Norton S. Townshend on "The
Perfectability of the Human Race."[10] Bassett

[7] Elyria *Courier*, March 9, 1847, and *History of Lorain
County, Ohio* (Philadelphia, 1879), p. 314. See the picture of
the Elyria square in Howe, *Historical Collection of Ohio*, p. 314.
[8] Elyria *Courier*, June 26, 1849.
[9] *Ibid.*, April 11, 1848.
[10] *Ibid.*, Aug. 10, 1849; Feb, 29, 1848; March 7, 1848, *et passim*. In the spring of 1847 Bassett offered a reward for the re-
covery of the account book of the treasurer of the Natural History Society. *Ibid.*, April 6, 1847. Townshend, local physician
and veterinarian, abolitionist, and Free-soil politician, was the

seemed willing to practice his handwriting in any good and respectable cause. There is just sufficient hint of quixotism here to prepare the observer for his participation in the Gold Rush to California.

Elyria's chief handicap was, as everywhere on the frontier, the lack of adequate facilities for transportation. The roads were execrable; the bridges were in poor repair. Railroads were, for the most part, in the blueprint stage. Late in 1847 the leading businessmen held a meeting to consider the advisability of constructing plank roads to near-by towns and especially of digging a ship canal along the valley of the Black River from below the falls to Lake Erie, eight miles away. Elyria would thus become a lake port. Milan, thirty miles to the west on the Huron River, had brought prosperity to herself by the Milan ship canal; it was estimated that over two million dollars worth of goods had passed in and out of the port of Milan in the preceding year.[11] But the canal on the Black River was destined never to be built and Lorain County's port remained on the lake.

The village of Black River (now the city of Lorain), on the natural harbor at the mouth of

later sponsor of the agricultural course at Oberlin and professor of agriculture at Iowa State and Ohio State, when those institutions were founded. See the *Dictionary of American Biography*.

[11] Elyria *Courier*, Dec. 21 and 28, 1847.

the stream, had already developed somewhat as the port of Elyria and of the county generally. By this time it had some fifty houses, a number of forwarding establishments and stores, and a light-house built by the Federal government in the thirties.[12] A Columbus girl visiting her uncle in 1846, has left us in her diary some glimpses of what it was like at the time. Writing on August 11, 1846, from the widow's walk atop her uncle's house, she painted what was, to a downstate girl, a romantic scene: "Far away to the east is seen a steamer speeding on its way, leaving a long train of black curling smoke in its wake, while to the north, seemingly at the very verge of the horizon where water and sky are blended together, is a brig, all its white sails set, and another is nearing the harbor here . . . and lying at the pier is another one, its sails closely furled, its various ropes look-ing almost skeleton like. Near it the pier stretches far out into the lake and supports the light-house standing like a faithful sentinel to warn and guard." On another evening she reported strolling out to the end of the pier and watching the at-tendants light the "eight lamps which are kept burning there throughout every night."[13]

Here at Black River, as early as 1819, a fifty-

[12] Howe, *Historical Collections of Ohio*, p. 317, and U. S. Congress, House Ex. Documents, 23 Cong., 2 sess., Vol. X, No. 193, Dec. 27, 1834.

[13] Manuscript diary of Olive M. Brown, August to October, 1846, property of Mr. Ralph McCombs, Columbus, Ohio.

ton sloop had been built: in the thirties and forties shipbuilding had become an important industry, and Black River vessels "not a few, as good as the best" now sailed the lakes.[14] One of the chief shipbuilders was Captain Thomas Cobb. In 1847 he launched the three-masted schooner *Samuel Strong,* named for one of her chief owners, an Elyria physician. This ship and her launching are described briefly in a contemporary newspaper article. She was a staunch and tubby vessel of over 200 tons' burden, the deck 113 feet long and 23 feet 8 inches beam, "her timbers having been selected from choice qualities and trimmed entirely free from sap. They were well salted when put together, and the *Strong* has a coat of metallic cement paint on her bottom and on deck." The celebration was worthy of the event, with a noisy crowd in attendance and many celebrants "reeling to and fro."[15]

From 1845 to 1848 Captain L. D. Burnell was associated with Cobb in building a number of ships. In the former year they built the schooner *John Erwin,* in 1847 the steam-propeller *Delaware* and the brig *Eureka,* and in 1848 the propeller *Ohio.*

The *Eureka,* which was to sail to California,

[14] *History of Lorain County,* p. 215, and D.T.B. to "Friend Bliss," Black River, Sept. 18, 1847, in the Elyria *Courier,* Sept. 21, 1847.

[15] Undated item from the Cleveland *Herald* copied in the Elyria *Courier,* Sept. 14, 1847.

had an 137-foot keel and 26-foot beam. She was
listed as a brig; that is, she had two masts with
square sails plus jib and spanker. Doubtless her
timbers, too, were carefully selected and "well-
salted" and her deck painted with "metallic cement paint." Being larger than the *Samuel Strong,*
she must have made a bigger splash when she hit
the waters of the Black River and the celebrants
must have been pretty numerous and normally
bibulous.[16]   From our knowledge of her notable
career we assume favorable auspices at her
launching.

Elyria, at this time, boasted two weekly newspapers, the *Courier* and the Lorain County *Argus,*
the *Courier* being the more useful and now the
more available. The Elyria *Courier* was edited
until 1848 by Philemon Bliss, abolitionist, lawyer,
Freesoil politician, and for many years after 1849
by George G. Washburn. In its columns were reported some of the events (though the omissions
are exasperating) which went to make up village
life (though nothing ever happened, of course) in
the Western Reserve of Ohio in those days.[17]

[16] *History of Lorain County,* p. 215; J. B. Mansfield, *History
of the Great Lakes* (2 vols.: Chicago, 1899), I, 823; and an
article from the Quebec *Pilot* quoted in the Quebec *Gazette,*
Oct. 22, 1849.
[17] The only considerable file of the *Courier* available to the
author is in the Western Reserve Historical Society Library, but
this is sadly incomplete.   On the editorship, see the *Courier,*
May 9, 1848, and *History of Lorain County,* p. 60.   Copies of
the Lorain County *Argus* are even rarer.

"Considerable excitement" was said to have resulted from the course of lectures delivered by the
Reverend Thomas Lake Harris on the latest
methods of communicating with the dead.[18] It is
doubtful, however, whether the young men and
boys looked upon this as an authentic "happen-
ing." In the columns of the *Courier* Cyrus Bassett
announced many undoubtedly informing but less
exciting-sounding lectures to be delivered before
the Natural History Society. Apparently most
people preferred the unnatural to the natural, then
as now. Elyrians read in the *Courier* that a certain Jerome B. Wilson had been murdered on
River Street on a dark night in the fall of 1847.[19]
(One supposes that a few more murders would
have redeemed the town from its dreary reputation.) The Lorain County Fair was fully reported.
It seems to have drawn exhibitors and visitors
from miles around; the premiums were numerous
but not very large.[20] On the Fourth of July of
1847 a country boy burned his arm severely with
gunpowder; Dr. Townshend amputated.[21] On the
same Independence Day, Professor John Morgan
of Oberlin College delivered a lecture against war,
in which he roundly denounced the attack of the
United States on Mexico.[22] Doubtless, however,

[18] Elyria *Courier,* Dec. 28, 1847, and June 25, 1848. See the
sketch of Harris in the *DAB.*
[19] Elyria *Courier,* Nov. 2, 1847.
[20] *Ibid.,* Oct. 26, 1847.   [21] *Ibid.,* July 6, 1847.
[22] *Ibid.*

there was more general interest in the accounts of American victories and the report that General Kearney was "in command as governor of California" and that a company of American immigrants (the Donner party), headed for the valley of the Sacramento, had lost many of its members in the snows of the Sierras.[23]

The advertisements in the *Courier* are perhaps as revealing as the news items. Practically every issue carried a display ad of H. K. Kendall's cash-and-carry store, called the "Old Fortress," containing a cut showing a wagonload of enthusiastic customers riding behind unnaturally prancing horses, the words they were supposedly shouting rising in a cartoonist's balloon over their heads: "We are bound for the great bargains at the 'Old Fortress.' "[24] Another and smaller ad read:

Farmers, Take Notice
I want to buy your
Fat Cattle, Fat Calves
FAT SHEEP AND HOGS!
And anything that you intend for the Elyria Market,
for which I will pay the market price in
CASH
Please call at the Market two doors east of
Dr. DeWitt's Drug Store.
Schuyler Strong.[25]

Now, Schuyler Strong may have been prospering,

[23] *Ibid.,* July 20, 1846.
[24] Webber, *Early History of Elyria,* pp. 89-92, and **Elyria Courier,** *passim.*
[25] *Ibid.,* June 26, 1849.

but there must have been quicker and more romantic ways to get rich. Gold mining sounded much more glamorous than butchering, anybody would have agreed. Besides, there might be a shortage of experienced butchers in California.

And Elyria had its own bank. In 1844, though Polk was elected president of the United States by the Democrats, Democrat David Tod of Youngstown, running on an antibank platform, was defeated for governor of Ohio, and the probank Whigs were established in control of the state government. In 1845 they put through the Kelley Bank Act, which provided for state branch banks and for independent banks which were required to deposit government bonds with the state treasurer as partial security for the banknotes which they issued.[26] William A. Adair, who had been a forwarding and commission merchant in Cleveland for several years, organized the first bank in Elyria and Lorain County under this law. Heman Ely and Artemas Beebe were among the stockholders. The bank opened for business on August 16, 1847, and Adair, the first cashier, began passing out the crisp, exciting new banknotes bearing the promises to pay of "The Lorain Bank of Elyria."[27] In this position Adair came to know and be known

[26] E. H. Roseboom and F. P. Weisenberger, *A History of Ohio* (New York, 1934), pp. 225-226.

[27] *Peet's Directory of Cleveland, 1846-1847* (Cleveland, 1846), p. 135; Elyria *Courier,* April 13 and Aug. 31, 1847; and Mary Beebe Hall, *Reminiscences of Elyria, Ohio* (Elyria, 1900), p. 48.

among the men of affairs of Lorain County and came to know much of their business. He must have met Schuyler Strong, the butcher and livestock dealer, Milo Bennet, the blacksmith, and Eleazer Abbe. Of course, he was closely associated with Beebe and the Elys and made the acquaintance of Bassett and of the shipbuilders of Black River, Thomas Cobb and Captain L. D. Burnell. When the pews in the new Presbyterian church were auctioned off, Adair paid $145.00 (probably in banknotes) for a pew two-thirds of the way down the right-hand aisle in the center section, one row ahead of Artemas Beebe and his family and just across the aisle from one of the pews purchased by Heman Ely, Jr.[28]

He must have known Burnell at an early date, because Burnell's partner, Thomas Cobb, had christened one of his earlier schooners for him, the *W. A. Adair.*[29] It is a good bet that Adair was on hand for the launching of the *Eureka* in 1847. Naturally, he was in a good position to finance any business venture, and any venture having his backing was given prestige by that fact. It is a reasonable guess that the Elyria banker had an interest in the *Eureka* even before he announced his intention to use her to take a party of goldseekers to California.

[28] Pew plan of the Elyria Presbyterian Church for 1848 in the Ely Papers in the possession of the Lorain County Historical Society.
[29] *History of Lorain County,* p. 213.

1. An early photograph of the Black River near its mouth. A hulk has just been launched: the ways are visible to the left. (Copied by A. E. Princehorn from a print by Charles Scheide.)

3.

Along the Cuyahoga

THE passengers and crew who went to California aboard the good ship *Eureka* came from Michigan, New York, Canada, and various points in northern Ohio, but the largest single group was from Cleveland. From Cleveland the ship's doctor, A. S. Baldwin, was recruited; Edward Beardsley, who shipped as steward, had resided on Mandrake Lane in Cleveland; Orlando Cutter, Jr., was the son of one of Cleveland's well-known auctioneers; Henry Howe of 30 Ontario Street was a carpenter and maker of blinds; John M. Brown and his son George lived on St. Clair Street; from Cleveland

came at least two of the cabin boys, George Hickox
and Norton Stedman; Henry Lloyd, who had been
a mason and brewer, was a resident of Huron
Street; the Manxman James Skillicorn boarded at
a house on Erie Street; other Clevelanders on the
Eureka were the blacksmith Andrew Kinninmouth
and William Kewin, a pattern maker; Thomas
Jones, the local maker of tombstones, allowed two
of his sons to sail to California in the *Eureka*
around the Horn.   Of a total roster of between
seventy and eighty, over twenty came from Cleveland.

In 1831 Thomas Jones brought his family from
Herefordshire to Cleveland at the mouth of the
Cuyahoga. Cleveland, with something over a
thousand people at that time—a little larger than
Elyria—was not yet the metropolis of northern
Ohio, but only one of various hopeful villages.
Jones was a stone-cutter and monument maker,
and, as Cleveland grew and more people lived and
died there, Jones's business prospered.   By 1848,
when Cleveland had become the population center of the Western Reserve, Jones inserted a display advertisement in the city directory: "Cleveland Marble Factory, Thomas Jones and Sons,
Sepulchral Monuments, Mural Tablets, Head-
stones."[1]   Of Jones's sons (he had thirteen chil-

[1] *Smead and Cowles' General Business Directory of the City
of Cleveland for 1848-9* (Cleveland, 1848) , p. 111.

dren), some followed him in the monument business; the eldest, his namesake, became a leading citizen in the community in later years, and two others made their fortunes in the gold fields of California and Nevada.

The secret of Cleveland's rapid growth lay in the Ohio Canal, completed in the thirties, connecting the mouth of the Cuyahoga with the Ohio River at Beaver just below Pittsburgh and at Portsmouth at the mouth of the Scioto in southern Ohio. From the interior of the state, north and south of the summit at Akron, the snub-nosed hulks drawn by mules brought wheat and flour and other farm products. A good deal of coal, iron ore, and lumber was hauled between Pittsburgh and Cleveland. On this latter run, in the summer and fall of 1848, young James Abram Garfield was working on a barge as "bow boy."[2] The canal boats were loaded and unloaded in Cleveland at the basin down on the flats below the present Terminal Tower.

Cleveland's chief business was buying and selling the goods that came in and went out by canal and their transshipment to and from other lake ports by means of the swarm of schooners, brigs, barques, and steamers that crowded the harbor

[2] E. J. Benton, *Cultural History of an American City, Cleveland*, Part II, *During the Canal Days, 1825-1850* (Cleveland, 1944), pp. 13-14. On Cleveland's exports in 1842, see *Cleveland as It Is: A History of Cleveland and Statistical Exhibit . . . for the Year 1871* (Cleveland, 1872), p. 12.

near the river mouth. Here were often seen Black River vessels like the *Samuel Strong,* the *Delaware,* the *John Erwin,* and the *Eureka.* William Adair had been a produce shipper and commission merchant in Cleveland before he went into banking at Elyria.[3] Isaac Hewitt was another "forwarding merchant," and president of the Canal Bank, one of the five Cleveland banks organized under the Kelley Act of 1845. Just a few years later he had the then unrecognized distinction of giving young John D. Rockefeller his first business opportunity, a job as assistant bookkeeper.[4] Adair's and Hewitt's quarters were not far from each other on Merwin Street, on the flats inside a kink of the Cuyahoga, strategically located between the canal basin and the river.

But, though there was much business activity in the river valley, the city was largely on the gravelly plain above, gathered around the public square. The Cuyahoga County Court House was on the southwest quarter of the square, and before it at regular intervals and on special occasions the volunteer marching clubs drilled: the Ringgolders or Flying Artillery, the Cleveland German Guards, the German Yagers, and the Hibernian Guards.[5]

[3] *Smead and Cowles' Directory of Cleveland for 1848-9,* p. 35; *Peet's Directory of Cleveland, 1845-6* (Cleveland, 1845), and for *1846-7.*

[4] Allan Nevins, *John D. Rockefeller* (New York, 1940), pp. 97-98.

[5] *Smead and Cowles' Directory of Cleveland for 1848-9,* p. 18.

The Old Stone (Presbyterian) Church was on the north side. Fine Greek-revival homes, stores, and office buildings extended to the east and west along St. Clair, Euclid, and Superior streets. Jones's marble works was on Seneca Street (West Third Street) just one block west. The impressive new medical school on St. Clair at the corner of the present East Ninth Street was an object of great local pride. The Weddell House on Superior was the best-known hotel, the stopping place of many celebrities. Probably the editor of one of the city newspapers had the Weddell in mind when he bragged in 1849 that "some of our splendid hotels" provided bathing facilities. The lack of such lux·uries in other hostelries was partly compensated for by the City Bath House, also on Superior, where shower baths were 12½ cents, Turkish baths $1, and season tickets $7.50.[6]

Cleveland was still pretty raw. Not a street was paved, and sometimes Superior Street was "like a troubled sea," where wandering hogs kept the mud in a constant state of turbulence. The hogs were a menace. Just before Christmas, 1848, a porker invaded a butcher shop, stole a turkey, and gave up its prize only after the proprietor had chased it some distance down the street. In February of 1849 the *True Democrat* advised "pedes-

[6] *Daily True Democrat,* March 31 and June 8, 1949, in the *Annals of Cleveland.*

trians not to venture out except on errands of mercy" until the mud dried up or froze.[7] This must have been prudent advice, especially for those inclined to walk out after dark, because gas lights were not introduced in Cleveland until the very end of that year.

Despite conditions underfoot, the town was often the scene of much activity. On market days the farmers came into town from many parts of rural northeastern Ohio, their wagons well loaded, considering the condition of the roads, with apples, butter, eggs, lard, oats, potatoes, dried fruit, and boiled cider. After selling out, they thronged the wooden sidewalks, visiting the shops and taverns, giving the place a very lively appearance. They hitched their teams on Euclid and around the Square, where, according to some complainants, the horses chewed the bark from the spindling shade trees.[8] On other days the auctioneers took possession of Superior Street and sold all sorts of "traps and calamities," while organ grinders "made music for the million." The dean of Cleveland auctioneers was Orlando Cutter, who had become an established institution in the years since 1825, when he first arrived in town. In the summer of 1849 he moved from Superior to new quarters on

[7] *Daily True Democrat*, Dec. 23, 1848, Feb. 27, April 16, July 29, Sept. 7, Dec. 8, 1849.
[8] *Ibid.*, April 13, 18, 1849.

Bank Street just across from the Weddell House. "The people will flock around him on August 15 and 16," predicted the *True Democrat*, "to buy goods as usual." Cutter's son, Orlando, Jr., was learning the business—the proper come-on, the right intonation,[9] but he was restless and eager to break away from parental domination and strike out on his own. He was ripe for a voyage to the Gold Fields.

Cleveland was growing rapidly. The town of six thousand of 1840 had doubled its population by 1847, and seventeen thousand inhabitants were listed for Cleveland by the census takers in 1850. (This number does not include the six thousand of Ohio City just across the river to the west.) Over a quarter were foreign born. In 1847, 20 per cent were of German birth and nearly 10 per cent natives of England. Many Irish lived in the poorer quarters, and there were closely knit colonies of Manxmen and Scots—the Society of St. Andrew, made up of Scots, was one of the most active social and charitable organizations in the city. Drunkenness, disease, squalor, and want were all too common among the newer arrivals, particularly the Irish, and some of the charitably minded women joined in the Martha Washington and Dorcas societies to solicit contributions and

[9] *Ibid.*, April 9, Aug. 8, 1849; Oct. 2, 1850, and Cleveland *Directories*.

dispense gifts of food and clothing to the indigent, the sick, and the aged.[10]

The coming of so many immigrants was a factor in the rapid expansion of Catholic, German Protestant, and other churches. There were twenty-one congregations altogether: Methodists, African Methodists, Wesleyans, Disciples, Jews, Congregationalists, Lutherans, Roman Catholics, etc. The Adventists had been waiting for the end of the world since 1843. A Bethel Mission Church was especially provided to save the souls of the down-and-out canawlers and the lake seamen. In April of 1849 a "large multitude" gathered on the lake front to watch the Baptists immerse a class of converts in the waves of Lake Erie.[11] The Presbyterian Old Stone Church not only enjoyed a strategic location on the square but probably had the most well-to-do congregation, though in this the Episcopalians rivaled the Presbyterians. The Episcopal Bishop of Ohio, Charles P. McIlvaine, was an evangelical, and in 1846-1847 he encouraged a "low-church" group to secede from the "high-church" Trinity Parish. The seceders organized a new parish called St. Paul's. The resulting controversy was bitter and alienated Trinity from

[10] Howe, *Historical Collections of Ohio*, p. 125; Benton, *Cultural History of Cleveland*, pp. 20-21; the Elyria *Courier*, Nov. 16, 1849, and the *Daily True Democrat*, Jan. 23, Nov. 17, 1849, *et passim* in the *Annals of Cleveland*.

[11] *Ibid.*, April 24, 1849. See Benton, *Cultural History of Cleveland*, pp. 28-32 on churches in Cleveland in this period.

their bishop for some years to come. The communicants of St. Paul's at first met in a hired hall but in 1849 undertook the construction of their own place of worship, a short distance up Euclid from the square at the intersection of Sheriff Street, the present East Fourth.[12] The building was well on the way to completion when it caught fire in the very early morning of Friday, August 3, 1849.

It was an exciting thing to see the fire companies run with their "fire engines"—the hand-pumper type, of course. It was, indeed, a form of sport, and there were many side bets made as to whether the Eagle, the Cataract, the Saratoga, the Phoenix, or Number Six would get its hose into one of the street-corner reservoirs first. A teenager by the name of Newton Holt had set fire to a schoolhouse woodshed, and apparently the results were satisfactory: he eventually confessed that he had set a number of other fires before that August second when he and a confederate crept into the shell of the deserted and still skeletal St. Paul's church.[13] It did make a "raree" show. The flames quickly leaped up to the roof and to the

[12] Sketch of Charles Pettitt McIlvaine in the *Dictionary of American Biography,* and George F. Smythe, *A History of the Diocese of Ohio until the Year 1918* (Cleveland, 1931), pp. 244-246 and 285-286.

[13] Holt's confession is quoted by "P" in a letter to the Editor of the *Plain Dealer,* Dec. 31, 1849.

tower. Fire bells rang and crowds poured down Euclid Avenue.

Eagle, Cataract, and Number Six reached a reservoir at about the same time; both Eagle and Number Six got their hoses in. But the fire was so far from any reservoir that it was necessary for several engines to relay the water from one to another, and there was chaotic lack of agreement as to the position in line. The Eagle Company refused to give water to Cataract; so Cataract went to another reservoir. Phoenix came up and was refused water by Number Six, but hooked up with Eagle. Number Six stayed at the reservoir. As the fire chief was out of town, the assistant fire chief took charge and finally persuaded Number Six to get in line behind Phoenix and Eagle, but the three together could not reach the fire. Cataract and Saratoga were now at other reservoirs. "About this time," reported the *True Democrat,* "St. Paul's was so far consumed that its tower fell across Euclid St." After three quarters of an hour the five engines were all hitched together and water was turned on a house near the ruined church.

The newspapers cried out against the tragic mismanagement. St. Paul's parish later built another tall-spired Gothic building on the same site. Newton Holt must have felt that he had gotten his money's worth. But some people suspected that arson was involved. As for Holt, wouldn't it be better to get out of Ohio before suspicion pointed to him? It would be hard to catch a fellow once he reached California. Here was another motive for joining in the Gold Rush.[14]

Cleveland's three daily papers covered sensational local events like the burning of St. Paul's and the discovery of the corpse of an unknown man in the river near Hewitt's warehouse. Much space in the four pages of each issue was devoted to state and national politics. Each newspaper had its easily identifiable political allegiance: Josiah Harris' *Herald* was Whig and generally conservative; the *Plain Dealer,* edited by John H. Gray, was the official Democratic organ; the *Daily True Democrat* was left-wing and Free Soil.

The big stories in these as in other American newspapers of the time were the Mexican War, the Gold Rush, the national election of 1848 and its preliminaries, the murder of Dr. George Parkman by Professor J. W. Webster of Harvard, the epidemic of cholera, and P. T. Barnum's importation of Jenny Lind. Everyday life is reflected most fully by the advertisements, supplemented by occasional "personals" and letters to the editor. The telegraph was just beginning to be used in getting

[14] For descriptions of the fire see *True Democrat,* Aug. 4, 1849, and the *Daily True Democrat,* Aug. 7, 1849. The names of the fire companies are given in *Smead and Cowles' Directory of Cleveland for 1848-1849,* p. 17.

news from other American communities, but
"latest advices" from Europe were, of course, weeks
or months old. Pope Pius IX left Rome on November 25, 1848, on account of the popular up-
rising, but it was not until February 22, 1849, that
the Cleveland *Daily True Democrat* reported that
"His Holiness has 'absquatulated' from the Vati-
can, or in vulgar Latin he has vamosed from the
Eternal City."

The presidential campaign of 1848 was an exciting one, locally as well as nationally. General
Lewis Cass, the Democratic candidate, paid a visit
to Cleveland, made a brief speech, and participated
in a parade. Eloquent old Tom Corwin appeared
in behalf of General Zachary Taylor. During his
speech some Mexican war veterans hanged and
burned an effigy of him. Thomas Jones, the marble cutter, joined with Edward Wade, Thomas
Bolton, and other leading citizens to call a meeting
to repudiate both Democrats and Whigs and send
delegates to a state Free Soil convention. Just
before the election, "Prince" John Van Buren addressed a Free Soil rally in behalf of his father, the
Free Soiler candidate for president. The *Daily
True Democrat* found him "truthful, eloquent and
impressive,"[15] but the Whig and Democratic papers
were not so complimentary.

[15] *Daily True Democrat,* June 12, 16, Sept. 15, and Oct. 27,
1848, in the *Annals of Cleveland.*

The Yankee reform element kept the pot of discussion boiling in off years as well as during political campaigns. In 1849 the Free Soilers sponsored a great "Celebration of the Anniversary of the Northwest Ordinance" in a big tent on the square, over the center pole of which waved a banner bearing the inscription: "The Ordinance of 1787; God, Liberty and Our Country." John Van Buren spoke again. In May of the same year the Baptist Church was packed to hear Horace Greeley deliver his already much-practiced lecture on Temperance. In the fall, John Hawkins, the Washingtonian teetotaler, horrified the uninitiated and inexperienced with his realistic descriptions of delerium tremens.[16]

Clevelanders' appetites for excitement might also be further appeased by attending a performance by "Young Alexander, the celebrated French Magician from Paris . . . the greatest necromancer in the World." Or they could join the large audience which went to see the Burr brothers give their demonstration of mesmerism; one evening "Several Ladies were on the stand, completely controlled." In May, 1848, Tom Thumb, the famous Barnum midget, was exhibited for four nights at Empire Hall. Dioramas and panoramas (storytelling paintings, the predecessors of the movies) dealt with current or historic, but always sensa-

[16] *Ibid.*, May 19, 23, July 16, Sept. 12, 15, 1849, in the *Annals.*

tional, subjects. Among those shown were "The
Burning of Moscow" ("richly worth the time . . .
the ventriloquism is admirable"), a panorama of
the Mexican War "occupying 21,000 feet of can-
vass," and the "Murder of Joe Smith."[17]

Music was furnished by the Empire Minstrels
(typical blackface), the Hutchinson Family (pur-
veyors of heart throbs and antislavery songs), and
Lowell Mason's musical conventions (which presented oratorios performed by local choruses).
Mrs. Mary Shaw Fogg gave a recital in December,
1849—the best a local critic could say was that she
was "a pure woman struggling . . . to educate a
child."[18] We have no information as to how many
Clevelanders thought it was worth twenty-five
cents to see this phenomenon.

Clevelanders seem to have been much interested in the drama. From April through October
of 1848 there were almost nightly performances at
the Apollo or New Theater, and occasional "read-
ings" of Shakespeare (*Hamlet, The Merchant of
Venice* and *"MacBeth"*) were given at the Weddell
House Hall. In October of 1849 a drama was
advertised under the title of *California Gold
Mines*.[19] But J. H. Gray of the *Plain Dealer* be-

[17] *Ibid.*, May 1, 2, 4, 16, 17, June 23, 1848, July 13, 16, Nov.
2, 6, 7, and Dec. 12, 1849, in the *Annals*.
[18] *Ibid.*, Sept. 9, 19, Nov. 15, 20, 1848; April 19, 21, Dec. 13,
14, 18, 19, in the *Annals*.
[19] *Ibid.*, 1848 *passim*, May 19, June 25, July 9, 11, Oct. 16,
1849, etc., in the *Annals*.

lieved that the theater was "the hot bed of vice and immorality," and that parents should keep their children away unless they wanted more juvenile delinquency.[20]

In the summer of 1849 a terrible epidemic of Asiatic cholera cast its shadow over the whole nation. Men arose in the morning in apparent good health, were stricken with fearful agonies at midday, and lay in their coffins before sundown. On June 25 a young man traveling on the Mad River Railroad from Cincinnati to Sandusky became ill on the cars. He was taken into the home of a Sandusky doctor and later recovered. But after that dozens and then hundreds of Sanduskians were attacked by the disease, and apparently about four hundred died in the next three months. At least eighty corpses were buried in one long trench, the coffins piled two or three deep.[21]

There was something like a panic in many parts of northern Ohio. The Oberlin College commencement, usually held in August, was called off for the only time in the history of the institution. The papers contained many recommendations for prevention and cure: drink whisky or don't drink whisky, avoid exertion, take "Ginger Syrup" or laudanum and spirits of camphor. "General" Mathiot, head of the Ohio Sons of

[20] *Ibid.,* Oct. 31, 1849.
[21] H. L. Peeke, *The Centennial History of Erie County, Ohio* (Sandusky, 1925), pp. 85-97.

Temperance, took a whole spoonful of the laudanum and camphor. He died, but not of cholera. President Zachary Taylor set aside the first Friday of August as a day of "fasting, humiliation and Prayer." All people were called upon to "assemble in their respective places of worship" and "to implore the Almighty . . . to stay the destroying hand which is now lifted up against us." Though Newton Holt chose to open this day of prayer and intercession in Cleveland by burning down St. Paul's Church, its observance was apparently generally more appropriate and seemly.[22]

Other Ohio communities came charitably to the assistance of the stricken city of Sandusky. "The Ladies of Elyria, feeling deeply for the inhabitants . . . who have suffered from the ravages of cholera," invited "all the benevolent of the village and the neighborhood, to meet at the house of Judge Long, . . . and bring in such articles of bedding, clothing, money or provisions, as can best be spared," to be used for bereaved and destitute Sanduskians. Clevelanders donated two hundred dollars for the same purpose, and three doctors and four male nurses from Cleveland risked infection by volunteering to work in the epidemic center. One of these latter was William Halsey Doan, just twenty-one years old. He had graduated from

[22] The Oberlin *Evangelist,* July 4, 18, Aug. 1, 15, 29, 1849, and the Cleveland *Daily True Democrat,* July 3, 28, Aug. 2, 4, 1849, in the *Annals of Cleveland.*

Shaw Academy and, at the time, was studying in the law office of Hitchcock, Wilson, and Wade.[23]

By this time all Cleveland's young men, along with other American young men, knew that adventure, romance, wealth, and power awaited them on the shores of the Pacific in newly-acquired California. In September of 1849, Orlando Cutter, Jr., apprentice auctioneer; Newton Holt, arsonist; two sons of Thomas Jones, the up-and-coming maker of tombstones; Halsey Doan, law student and humanitarian; young Doctor Albert S. Baldwin; the Manxman James Skillicorn; and many other Clevelanders sailed for the land of gold on the Black River-built *Eureka*.

[23] The Lorain County *Argus*, Aug. 14, 1849; the *Daily True Democrat*, Aug. 1, 1849; Peeke, *Centennial History of Erie County*, p. 89; and P. M. Ladd, "W. H. Doan, Eulogy of His Life and Character," *Annals of the Early Settlers Association of Cuyahoga County*, No. XI, pp. 395-397.

4.

Oh, Susannah!

On February 2nd, Ground Hog Day, 1848, in the suburb of Mexico City called Guadalupe Hidalgo, the treaty was signed which gave California to the United States. The "manifest destiny" of the nation was thus in part revealed even to those who had not recognized it before, though no one could yet foresee the vast orange groves, the "Top of the Mark," Hollywood, or Santa Monica. Here at least was the beginning of the fruition of Old Zach Taylor's victory at Buena Vista, of Scott's miraculous expedition from Vera Cruz to Chapultepec, of Stephen Kearny's conquest of New

Mexico, and of the weird combination of internal unrest and outside invasions of California itself. The old Ground Hog must certainly not have seen his shadow; it must have been an unusually cloudy day in the sunshine land, for it was not long, as the world wags, before the full American summer would begin in California.

Just nine days before the signing of the treaty, James Wilson Marshall, a native of New Jersey who had moved to the West Coast before the war, had discovered specks of gold in the tail race of a sawmill he was building on the south fork of the American River at Coloma. Marshall had tried to keep his secret, but soon after, Sam Brannan, a Mormon storekeeper from near-by Sacramento (then Sutter's Fort), had hurried down to the quiet little Spanish-American village of San Francisco and rushed into town waving a phial filled with yellow flakes and shouting, "Gold! Gold! Gold from the American River!" Whether he spoke in just these words or not, and no one at the time and place seems to have recorded them, Sam Brannan's proclamation echoed over the bay and against the hills. *Gold,* said the waters of the Pacific. *Gold,* said the sun setting beyond Fremont's Golden Gate. *Gold. Gold.* The magic word was heard in Sonora, in Peru, in Hawaii, in Australia, in France. Young men everywhere were awakened by the call—in New England, in Missouri, on the Square before the courthouse in Elyria, by the banks of the ship canal at Milan, beside the Cuyahoga, in Chautauqua County in New York, on the farms of Trumbull and Wayne counties in Ohio. *California. Gold. California.*

On August 29, 1848, the New York *Journal of Commerce* had run a sensational story. According to this account, gold could be picked out of the earth here and there all over California with no trouble at all. People were digging it up everywhere, so it was said, like a herd of hogs rooting up "ground nuts" in the forest. More stories from the new Eldorado appeared in various eastern papers in August, September, October, and November, but the great excitement did not come in the "States" until December.[1]

In July Col. Richard B. Mason, who had succeeded Kearny in military command and as acting governor in California, had visited the gold diggings along the American River in company with the then Lieutenant William Tecumseh Sherman. From information thus secured Mason prepared a circumstantial account of the discovery and the progress of exploitation of the gold deposits. This report he sent to the Secretary of War along with a "tea caddy" filled with samples of actual Cali-

[1] There is, of course, a very extensive literature. See especially John Walton Caughey, *Gold Is the Cornerstone* (Berkeley, 1948), and Owen C. Coy, *Gold Days* (Los Angeles, 1929). There is a useful sketch of James Wilson Marshall in the *Dictionary of American Biography.*

fornia nuggets. This box of gold was put on exhibition at the War Office, where Americans could feed their hungry eyes upon the actual article.

On December 5 James K. Polk sent to Congress his regular message on the state of the Union. It was natural that in it he should point with pride to the achievements of his presidency. The American citizen army, he declared, had won the plaudits of the world with its renowed exploits. As a result of the new acquisitions of territory "the United States are now estimated to be nearly as large as the whole of Europe." He could now announce officially that the rumors of the existence of unprecedented quantities of gold in California had been "corroborated by the authentic reports of officers in the public service." Along with the message he sent to Congress the full text of Mason's statement.

The Message was reprinted in full in the Cleveland *Plain Dealer* on Thursday and Friday, December 7 and 8. It appeared also in the *Herald* and in many other local Ohio papers. The Painesville *Telegraph* had it in the December 13 issue. Mason's report was presented as a kind of sequel a few days later. Thus in all the newspapers the signal was given which started the race for California.

The *Plain Dealer* sounded the bugle call editorially:

That portion of the President's Message which treats of the Gold Region, will be read with thrilling interest. It will set on fire the young men of the country. The Yankee spirit will be aroused, and a rush will be made to this newly discovered Eldorado. If 40,000 young men, lured by the fancied wealth of Mexico, would climb, amid shot and shell, the hills of Monterrey, storm the castle of San Juan, brave the pass of Cerro Gordo, with how much more alacrity will they fly to a country all their own, where no peril attends the enterprize, and whose boundless harvests of gold are certified to by the president of the Nation?

Here was the popular evaluation of the President's Message. It was the official certification of the existence of "boundless harvests of gold" in California. Let all the young men be "set on fire." Let the "Yankee spirit be aroused."

This was an enterprise for which the Yankees were especially qualified, according to the *Plain Dealer:*

What a god-send . . . are these native gold deposits. They are better than all the Wilmot Provisos and newspaper thunder forged by all the political vulcans of the land, to *prevent* the extension *of slavery.* The *slave-holder cannot leave his slaves, thank God, to go there himself, and he dares not take them with him* . . . . But the Yankees—the freemen of the North are not encumbered with any such 'peculiar' property. They want but a day's notice to dispose of their goods and chattels, shake hands with their friends, and be off. They will appropriate that country to themselves, and in less than two years will claim pre-emption rights to every rod of it.[2]

[2] Cleveland *Plain Dealer,* Dec. 8, 1848.

But there must be no delay, or others might reap that golden harvest.

Within a month a party of goldseekers from Sandusky was on its way by the overland route. Gold mining companies were organized in Conneaut and East Cleveland. In March parties left Akron and Painesville. On March 26 sixteen young men marched out of Painesville, cheered on their way by the applause of their assembled townsmen. They floated down the Beaver and the Ohio to St. Louis, and from St. Louis traveled "by mule" to Independence and thence across the plains and over the mountains by the same sturdy means of locomotion. The Bellevue Mining Company, with four wagons, two tents, and a considerable supply of provisions, went by way of St. Joseph. Twelve young Clevelanders, organized as the "California Auriferous Mining Company," started west on the last day of May. In June a caravan left Milan to cross the continent for the diggings. By the dozens and half-dozens they marched away from every county in the Western Reserve.[3]

Some discordant voices were raised. The *Plain Dealer,* as a Democratic paper, would be expected to follow the Administration line, but the Free

[3] Robert Thomas, "Buckeye Argonauts," *Ohio State Archaeological and Historical Quarterly,* LIX (July 1950), 256-269; Painesville *Telegraph,* March 28, 1849; Cleveland *Daily True Democrat,* June 2, 1849; Milan *Tribune,* June 20, 1849.

Soil *Daily True Democrat* was incredulous at first. "We trust that our readers will not all start for California," it warned Clevelanders the day after the publication of the President's message. They should beware of "the glittering, golden bubble message of President Polk." "All is not gold that glitters; and all things in Mr. Polk's Message should not be taken as true."[4] A meeting of the Painesville Lyceum "at the Brick School House" in mid-January gave the citizens of Lake County a chance to hear both sides, for the question discussed was "Will the discovery of gold mines in California ultimately prove beneficial to the people of the United States?"[5] Thirty-five miles west of Cleveland, students of Oberlin College at a meeting of one of their literary societies debated the topic: "The recent discovery of Gold in California a curse (or a blessing) to our Country."[6] Probably the chief result of such discussion was to give additional publicity to the Land of Gold.

Authors, publishers, and booksellers seized the opportunity to present the public with a variety of more or less pertinent volumes. Among these were many emigrant's guides and miner's manuals. In Cleveland Younglove and Company advertised a new edition of Charles Wilkes's *Narrative* of ex-

[4] Quoted in the *Annals of Cleveland* from the *Daily True Democrat,* Dec. 8, 1849.

[5] Painesville *Telegraph,* Jan. 10, 1849.

[6] R. S. Fletcher, *A History of Oberlin College* (2 vols.; Oberlin, 1943), II, 771.

plorations of the Pacific and "Jeremiah Saddlebag's *Journey to the Gold Region.*" The latter was a "comic book" of the Gold Rush published in Cincinnati, selling for twenty-five cents. The Cleveland *Daily True Democrat* carried in March of 1849 a notice of *"Signor D'Alvear's Goldometer: The Gold Seeker's Guide; or Secret Art of Finding Mines of Gold, Silver, Iron, Lead, Copper, Coal and other Mineral Riches."* With this book on hand, if you didn't find gold you might, at least, find coal. Readers were assured that the Signor knew what he was talking about, though perhaps someone was confusing Italians and Spaniards. "Signor D'Alvear," potential purchasers were informed, "found gold on Sacramento River with his secret magnetic instrument 2 yrs. ago." The book cost one dollar. It is not clear whether a magnetic dowsing rod or "geiger counter" was included with the sale.[7]

At Boston, New York, Kansas City, and Cleveland, merchants were more than willing to sell supplies to outgoing miners: picks and shovels, Colt's revolvers, blankets, hard biscuits, salt meat, fantastic mining machinery, and money belts to carry gold in. Sheet music could be purchased:

[7] *Daily True Democrat*, March 22, June 6, Aug. 28, 1849, the latter two items as quoted in the *Annals of Cleveland.* On "Jeremiah Saddlebags," see Archer B. Hulbert, *Forty-Niners* (Boston, 1931), p. 61 n. For another story of a "Goldometer," see H. H. Bancroft, *California Inter Pocula* (California, 1888), pp. 387-388.

"The Sacramento Gallop," "The San Francisco Waltz," and "The Gold Digger's Waltz." Everybody was singing some one of the many new versions of Stephen Foster's "Oh, Susannah!"

> I'll scrape the mountains clean, old girl,
> I'll drain the rivers dry.
> I'm off for California. Susannah, don't you cry.

Once the great question, of whether to go was settled in the affirmative, one problem still remained: How do we get there? On December 11, 1848, when the excitement was just beginning, the *Plain Dealer* published a letter from "Honest Enquirers," who expressed the confusion and uncertainty which must have been in the minds of many venturesome young Ohioans. It is addressed to the editor.

> Mr. Gray: Not knowing of any person from whom I would be more likely to obtain the information which I wish, than yourself, I now take the liberty to enquire concerning the route to the gold regions of California. Which is the most expedient and direct route by land, or which would be the best port to ship from in case one go by water [?] And of the two ways, land and water, which would be the quickest and safest [?] Will you please answer these few questions in your paper, and much oblige a few Honest Enquirers.[8]

The prospective forty-niners had many routes to pick from. Some took passage on the new mail

[8] Cleveland *Plain Dealer,* Dec. 11, 1848.

steamers to Panama, traveled over the Isthmus by boat and burro, and then on to California by mail steamer again, if there happened to be space available. This was generally the quickest route, but the dangers and the inconveniences of the stay in a tropical land kept many from utilizing it. Some crossed the Gulf from New Orleans to Vera Cruz and then went across Mexico along difficult mountain paths to the west-coast ports of Acapulco or Mazatlan, and thence, by any ship that came by, north to San Francisco. Most Middlewesterners trekked directly west through American territory: southwest along the Santa Fe Trail and along the Gila, or up the Platte Valley and through South Pass by the much-rutted covered-wagon route past Salt Lake, along the Humboldt, and over the high passes of the Sierra Nevada. If this overland road was followed it was necessary to start fairly early in the season in order to get through the mountains before the snows came.

Goldseekers from New England and the East in general favored one of the sea routes: by Panama, Tehuantepec, or all the way by water around Cape Horn or through the Straits of Magellan. This was indeed a long way round, but to many from seaport towns who were unaccustomed to long-distance overland journeys and who looked upon the ocean as the great highway, it seemed like the easiest, the most natural, and the most comfortable way. Besides, this was the cheapest route for the transportation of heavy goods: hardware, lumber, dry goods, manufactured provisions, and machinery. The carpenter, the blacksmith, the general mechanic could take his tool with him more conveniently and at less expense. The printer could take his press. Many women and a large proportion of the professional men—doctors, ministers, lawyers—preferred this less arduous, but at least equally tedious, route.[9]

In the last weeks of 1848 and in the early months of 1849 hundreds of vessels of all sorts and conditions cleared from Boston and New York, bulging with the materials of Anglo-American civilization (from whisky and Bibles to shovels and playing cards) and crowded with purposeful and hopeful Yankee emigrants, all California bound.

[9] Among the best treatments of the emigration to California are Oscar Lewis, *Sea Routes to the Gold Field* (New York, 1949) ; Caughey, *Gold Is the Cornerstone,* pp. 57 to 158; Ralph P. Bieber, ed., *Southern Trails to California in 1849* (Glendale, 1937) ; William S. Ament, *Oxcart to Airplane: By Sea to California* (Los Angeles, 1929) ; John C. Parish, "By Sea to California," in J. F. Willard and C. B. Goodykoontz, *The Trans-Mississippi West* (Boulder, 1930) , and Raymond A. Rydell, *Cape Horn to the Pacific* (Berkeley, 1952) .

5.

Fresh Water Argonauts

WILLIAM A. ADAIR, the Elyria banker and former
Cleveland commission merchant, was not the kind
of man who would want to miss a great speculative
venture. As the news from California beat upon
his brain it germinated an idea—an idea that was
just daring enough to appeal to a generation willing to try anything. The idea was to send a ship
from the Great Lakes through the St. Lawrence to
the Atlantic and then around Cape Horn to California.

The success of the Erie Canal had impressed
the Canadians and inspired them to build a series

of canals which might compete for the great traffic which was pouring down to New York from the Middle West. The Welland Canal, connecting Lake Erie and Lake Ontario and bypassing Niagara Falls, was opened in 1829. Originally taking no vessels of more than 22 foot beam, it was rebuilt in 1846 supposedly to accommodate those of 26½ feet width. Canals of considerably greater capacity around the St. Lawrence rapids between Lake Ontario and Montreal were opened to traffic in 1848. So it was physically possible to sail a ship of medium tonnage from Lake Erie to the ocean by this date.[1]

But British and Canadian law prohibited the passage of foreign, including American, vessels through the St. Lawrence River. The United States had recognized the British right to close the river in the Jay Treaty of 1794. This restriction forced some commerce into the Erie Canal that might otherwise have used the Canadian route, and there was much agitation in Montreal, as well as in American ports like Detroit and Cleveland for its abandonment. The issue was further confused by the question of reciprocity between the United States and Canada and even by some talk of annexation. "The free navigation of the St. Lawrence first," said the Cleveland *Daily True*

[1] T. C. Keefer, "The Canals of Canada," in Royal Society of Canada, *Transactions . . . for the Year 1893* (Ottawa, 1894), Sec. III, pp. 25-50.

Democrat in April, 1849, "then if the people of
Canada say so, and Great Britain assents, annexation." Though, from the American point of view,
cautiously stated, such irresponsible comments
doubtless irritated patriotic Canadians and delayed
action. The St. Lawrence was not generally opened
to American shipping until a provision to that
effect was included in the Reciprocity Treaty of
1854.[2]

In the meantime, however, it was possible to
secure special permission for individual excep-
tions, and this Adair proposed to do. He appealed
to George Bancroft, the historian and at the time
United States minister to Great Britain, to inter-
vene with the British government in his behalf,
and on May 9, 1849, an official of the Privy Council wrote to Mr. Bancroft: "I am directed by the
Lords of the Committee of Privy Council for
Trade, to state to you, with reference to your ap-
plication on behalf of Mr. W. A. Adair to be
allowed to convey his Brig the 'Eureka' from the
Lakes, through the St. Lawrence to the Atlantic,
that under the circumstances mentioned, their
Lordships have directed that the necessary Instruc-

[2] George W. Brown, "The Opening of the St. Lawrence to
American Shipping," *Canadian Historical Review*, VII (March,
1926), 4-12; D. G. Creighton, *The Commercial Empire of the
St. Lawrence, 1760-1850* (Toronto, 1936), pp. 358-385; Gilbert
Norman Tucker, *The Canadian Commercial Revolution, 1845-
1851* (New Haven, 1936), pp. 115-135, and the Cleveland *Daily
True Democrat*, April 28, 1849, as cited in the *Annals of Cleve-
land* (Cleveland, 1938).

tions shall be forthwith transmitted to the col-
lectors of customs at Montreal and Quebec, to
comply with the wish of Mr. Adair."[3]

Captain L. D. Burnell, it will be recalled, was
one of the builders of the *Eureka*. Burnell of
Black River joined with Adair, the Elyrian, in
sponsoring a voyage of the *Eureka* to California.
Who in 1847, when the *Eureka* was christened,
could have guessed how appropriate its name was
to be? Or perhaps the name gave Adair the idea.

In July an announcement appeared in the
Plain Dealer under the heading "First and only
Vessel from the Lakes for San Francisco!" The
text read as follows:

> The Brig Eureka of Cleveland, L. D. Burnell,
> Master will sail on or about the 15th day of Septem-
> ber next, for the above port.
> The requisite permission has been obtained from
> the British Government to pass through the St. Law-
> rence into the Atlantic. The vessel will be rigged into
> a Barque, sheathed and fitted up with comfortable
> cabins, and everything else necessary to make the
> passage safe and agreeable. The services of an ex-
> perienced captain, familiar with the route, will be
> obtained to take charge during the voyage out.
> This is decidedly the cheapest, and the safest, and
> the best route to the Gold Diggings. A rare chance is
> here offered to those who wish to make a very large
> fortune out of a small one.

[3] The National Archives, Record Group No. 59, General
Records of the Department of State, Diplomatic Despatches,
Great Britain, vol. 59.

3. The second Beebe House, opened in 1848. To the rear, the Presbyterian Church, of 1848, and the City Hall, of post-Civil War construction. (From a print in the possession of the author.)

Cabin fare was to be $200.00. "Each passenger
to provide and care for his own bed and bedding,
and to be allowed to carry free as baggage, one
barrel bulk." Additional freight might be carried
at five dollars per barrel. Adair agreed to lend
money to those needing credit if "approved security" was available. Agents were listed at Cleveland (I. L. Hewitt, Adair's former fellow commission merchant on Merwin Street), Buffalo, Milan,
Sandusky, Detroit, Chicago, Kingston, Montreal
and Pittsburgh. Adair was his own agent at Elyria.
Identical or similar advertisements appeared in the
Detroit *Daily Advertiser,* the Lorain *Argus,* and
the Cleveland *Daily True Democrat.*[4]

In midsummer the *Plain Dealer* reported that
preparations for sailing were well under way:

The Eureka is now in this port fitting up for California, and will sail as advertised. Capt. D. P. Nick-
erson is superintending the outfit, than whom no
better man can be found to take charge of a matter
of this kind, and the vessel being new and well built,
she will be put in the most perfect order for sea. She
has authority to pass through the British waters to
the sea, for we have *seen the documents* signed and
sealed by the proper authorities. Now whoever wants
to immortalize himself, sail half round the world, exchange the coming winter for a southern summer, and
find himself some fine morning entering the bay of
San Francisco with the golden mountains full in view,
all for two hundred dollars; here is a chance and
possibly the only one you will have in a life time.

[4] Cleveland *Plain Dealer,* July 16, 1849.

Several of the first young gentlemen of this city have spoken berths; and applications are being made from abroad.[5]

And appetites for gold were freshly whetted as the news was received that the steamer *Falcon* from Panama had docked at New Orleans with $170,000 of California dust.[6]

Notices in September warned that would-be gold miners who wanted to travel by this all-water route would have to act at once. "The Barque EUREKA is now taking in her Freight," declared Adair in the *Plain Dealer* on September 15, "and will positively sail on the 24th inst., wind and weather permitting. Room for a few more passengers. Apply at once." In the same issue the newspaper gave an editorial puff to the home-town enterprise under the headline, "Ho! for the Gold Diggings":

By advertisement, in another column it will be seen the fine barque *Eureka* is positively to sail to California on the 24th, just a week from next Monday. This is a capital chance for anyone who has the gold fever. We know several who are going on her, among our citizens, and we will guarantee that if good company, a first rate sail craft, and an excellent appointment of officers and crew, can make a voyage pleasant, this will be.

[5] Quoted from the *Plain Dealer* in the Lorain County *Argus*, Aug. 14, 1849.
[6] Lorain County *Argus*, August 14, 1849. (A copy of this issue is in the possession of the Lorain County Historical Society.)

Even the Free Soil and querulous *Daily True Democrat* gave its blessing: "Let our young men who have resolved to go, embrace this fine opportunity. None so good will offer from the West."[7]

The vessel had now been rerigged as a barque, that is with three masts, square rig on the foremast and main mast, fore-and-aft on the mizzen mast—this instead of the two-mast rigging of the brig. Two cabins were built on the main deck, the larger with sixty berths built around the side for the single males and the smaller for the family groups.[8] No steerage passage was provided, the hold and between decks being given over to freight and provisions.

Adair himself did not plan to go with the ship, but sent L. D. Burnell as supercargo. William Monroe, who was said to have "made several voyages round Cape Horn," was retained as captain in command. A later story from the Quebec *Mercury* described him as "a thorough seaman, remarkable for his urbane and gentlemanly bearing." Dr. Albert S. Baldwin of Cleveland was ship's physician and surgeon. Edward Beardsley, a young bookkeeper of Cleveland, was made steward.[9]

[7] Detroit *Daily Advertiser*, July 18, 1849, quoted in the Detroit *Daily Advertiser Digest*, 1849, pp. 181-182; the Lorain County *Argus*, Sept. 18, 1849; the Cleveland *Daily True Democrat*, Sept. 12, 1849, quoted in the *Annals of Cleveland* (Cleveland, 1938).

[8] Description in the San Francisco *Alta California*, Oct. 21, 1850.

[9] The Quebec *Mercury*, Nov. 19, 1951, quoted in the Cleveland *Plain Dealer*, Nov. 20, 1849.

About thirty people from Cleveland signed up·
for the voyage. These included the Jones boys,
John P. and Henry A., sons of the well-known
tombstone manufacturer, Orlando Cutter, Jr.,
whose father was the leading auctioneer, and William Halsey Doan. Doan was studying law in the
summer of 1849 when not engaged in nursing cholera victims in Sandusky. There were several teen-
agers from Cleveland: George Hickox, Newton
Holt and his confrere, W. S. Parker, and two of
the four cabin boys, Thomas Smith and Norton
Stedman. Holt and Parker were anxious to go by
the most expeditious means, before the strong arm
of the law caught up with them.[10]

There had been much interest in California in
Milan from the beginning of the year as indicated
by the number of items on the Gold Rush appearing in the Milan *Tribune*. Three men from Milan
took passage on the *Eureka*. Most prominent of
these was Samuel Grosh, local retailer and active
worker in the Whig party. As early as May he
had announced the closing out of his stock:

[10] On the passengers, officers, and crew see lists in the Cleveland *Daily Herald*, Sept. 25, 1849, and the *Plain Dealer*, Sept.
26. Essential is the passenger list in the manuscript diary of
Eleazer Abbe, particularly because of the many serious typographical errors in the newspaper lists. Abbe gives the occu-
pations of all passengers. On W. H. Doan see Alfred A. Doane,
The Doane Family (Boston, 1910), pp. 329-330, and P. H. M.
Ladd, "W. H. Doan," *Annals of the Early Settlers of Cuyahoga
County*, No. XI, pp. 395-397.

OPH FOR CALIFORNIA

Open for Six Months!

SAML. GROSH, late with C. S. Meeker, is now opening at the Store in Lockwood Block, recently occupied
by G. Barney, a large Stock of New and Fresh Goods,
Embracing all kinds of

Domestic and Fancy Dress Goods,

GROCERIES,

HARD WARE, CROCKERY,

NAILS, GLASS

Boots and Shoes, Hats, Caps

BONNETS, &,

Which are to be sold for *Ready Pay only.*

Profit or no profit, all must be sold.

Lawns and Ginghams, (fast colors,) 12¢ per yard
Prints   do.   4 to 6¢ do
Sheetings,   5 7 and 8¢ per yard.
Sugar   16 to 13 lbs. for $1.
Teas   20 to 50¢ per lb.
Coffee   12 to 14 lbs. for $1.

And all other Goods at equally low prices.

Milan, May 23, 1849.   SAML. GROSH[11]

Only one man was on the *Eureka* from Painesville. He was a farmer, Colbert Carthron Huntington, twenty-nine years old, a descendant of the
first pioneer family of the area.[12] W. W. Culver,
of Green Creek, Ohio, listed himself as "Counsel-
lor-at-Law." W. B. Corey was also from Green
Creek. The loss of these ambitious young men
must have blighted all hope for Green Creek's

[11] Milan *Tribune,* Sept. 12 and 19, 1849.
[12] Huntington Family Association, *The Huntington Family
in America* (Hartford, 1915) , p. 589.

becoming a prosperous metropolis. Freeman Eggleston of Independence was a contractor; E. W. Williams, carriage maker, came from Middlebury, then an independent village but later absorbed into the city of Akron. William Stacey had been a Michigan farmer.

Elyria contributed Cyrus E. Bassett, Lorain County recorder, Milo Bennett, blacksmith and one of the village trustees,[18] the butcher Schuyler Strong, and Eleazer Abbe. Posterity is especially indebted to Abbe, because he kept a diary.

There were eight woodworkers among the passengers. These included Huntington, young Henry A. Jones, and Henry Howe, listed in the 1846 Cleveland directory as a maker of window blinds. John M. Brown and his son George S., of 83 St. Clair Street, Cleveland, were both carpenters. Two—George B. Harvey of Cleveland and F. J. Skear of Royalton—were ship carpenters. W. D. Lewis of Milan said he was a carpenter and *astronomer!*

Several were workers in metals, including four blacksmiths: Bennett of Elyria, the Scotsman Andrew Kinninmouth of Cleveland, and two others. The Cleveland Manxman James Skillicorn was a boilermaker. James F. Bryan was a coppersmith; William Kewin and George S. Clute were

[18] Elyria *Courier,* April, 1847, and *History of Lorain County,* p. 113.

pattern makers; David Nelson was a moulder—all of these were from Cleveland.[14]

Robert Taylor of Cleveland was a baker; Henry Lloyd was the son of a mason and had worked at that trade and also as a brewer. The Lloyds lived at 70 Huron Street in Cleveland. John P. Jones was listed as a bookkeeper, though like the rest, he would willingly be a gold miner. There were two tailors and one tanner on board.

Most of the adventurers did not take their families, if they had any. Eleazer Abbe left his wife and children in Elyria. But J. F. Bryan was accompanied by his wife and stepson, and F. J. Skear's wife and son went with him.

Many Yankee forty-niners were as much interested in the possibility of large profits from the sale of goods in short supply on the California market as in mining. What difference did it make *how* they got rich? The *Eureka* carried a mixed cargo, probably mostly owned by Adair and Burnell. The largest single item was lumber, fifty thousand board feet of it. Also included were 125 wooden doors ready to hang on hastily erected buildings in San Francisco or interior California towns. The 37 barrels of paint would help make those structures more presentable, if anyone was going to bother with that sort of thing.

[14] On Howe, the Browns, and some other Clevelanders see *Peet's Directory of Cleveland, 1846-1847.*

Of hardware the *Eureka* carried 169 stoves with stove pipe and elbows and a complement of tin boilers and tin ovens. Stoves constituted a large factor in shipments from the East to California in early Gold-Rush days. In her hold also was a steam engine for a sawmill and sawmill fixtures. Among the mechanics in the cabin were undoubtedly some who were prepared to set up the mill.[15]

The supply of provisions for sale, apart from those intended for consumption on the voyage, included fifty barrels of flour and twenty of corn meal, five hundred bags of salt, ten boxes of pickles, and a ton of bologna sausage.

The five tons of grindstones probably came from Henry Baldwin's famous Berea quarries. Maybe the four cases of cigars were intended as bribes for Spanish American port officials.

On the evening of Monday, September 24, the *Eureka* was moved down the Cuyahoga to the pier near the mouth of the river. Just before noon of the next day, as a large crowd on shore cheered her, she cast off and was hauled out into deeper water by the steamer *Hendrick Hudson,* another product of the Black River ways. She did not make sail, however, until the twenty-sixth. As the *Plain Dealer* put it: "Her crew as is usual, with

[15] There are three available lists of the cargo. The discrepancies between them are minor. The "Lake Record" in the *Plain Dealer,* Sept. 26, 1849, and the Montreal *Pilot* as quoted in the *Plain Dealer,* Oct. 26, 1849, and in the Quebec *Gazette,* Oct. 22, 1849.

Sailors bound on a long voyage had to take the parting hand, and perhaps the parting glass, with so many of their old comrades that at sailing time they were *non est inventus.* So the . . . gold-seekers had to hold over one night more, in the land of Golgotha, before sailing to their new Eldorado."[16] Henry Howe's father presented him with a cane as a going-away present.

On the evening of Thursday, September 27, the vessel reached the entrance of the Welland Canal, where "all the boys" were reported to be still "in good spirits," despite the fact that near this point the *Eureka* collided with the steamer *London* and damaged her considerably. The St. Catharines *Journal* found it a "gratifying sight to see a three-masted vessel passing through our Canal, from the upper lakes to the Pacific."[17] Here Howe mislaid his cane, but recovered it.

The narrowest lock in the Welland was supposed to be twenty-six feet and six inches wide; the *Eureka* had a twenty-six foot beam. Supposedly she should have no difficulty in slipping through. One lock, however, was apparently below specifications, and the width of the *Eureka* had therefore to be reduced a few inches in order to get her past. The Montreal *Pilot* found this

[16] This account of the clearing of the *Eureka* is based on the stories in the Cleveland *Daily Herald,* Sept. 25, and the *Plain Dealer,* Sept. 26. The second report corrects the errors of prophecy in the first.
[17] *Plain Dealer,* Oct. 2, 1849.

"truly mortifying," as the voyage was looked upon
as a demonstration of the practicability of taking
ships to sea from the upper lakes. "Of what injury
would it be to Canada," the *Pilot* asked editorially,
"to have 500 or 600 American vessels passing down
to the ocean, and paying us tolls? Should we not
have the St. Lawrence free, whether we get Recip-
rocal Trade or not?"[18]

Not all of the passengers made the trip through
the St. Lawrence. For two Clevelanders the voyage
was abruptly interrupted. On the day the *Eureka*
sailed away from the mouth of the Cuyahoga, the
mayor offered a reward of $500 for the arrest or
evidence leading to "the conviction of the person
or persons, who have within the last 60 days set fire
to any building in this city." August 3, the date
of the burning of St. Paul's church, was well within
this interval.

A Buffalo police officer arrested Newton Holt
and William Parker on board the *Eureka* and
brought them back to Cleveland, where they were
lodged in the jail on the morning of October 9.
The trial of the young arsonists (Holt was only
nineteen) took place from October 23 to 28, and
was something of a local sensation, a good deal of
sympathy being expressed for them because of
their age. Edward Wade, brother of Congressman

[18] Quoted in the *Plain Dealer*, Oct. 26, and the Quebec
Gazette, Oct. 22, 1849. There seems to be a typographical error
in the figures on lock width as given in the *Plain Dealer* version.

Ben Wade and member of the firm to which Halsey Doan had been apprenticed, gave his services without charge for the boys' defense. The jury in the case was out from eleven in the evening of Saturday, October 27, to five o'clock Sunday morning, when they returned a verdict of guilty. Holt was sentenced to six years in the penitentary, where he later confessed. Cleveland editors were inclined to blame his crime on the lack of a city curfew and the demoralizing influence of the theater upon juveniles.[19] (Perhaps they had in mind such stories of violence as *Macbeth and Hamlet*.) It was too bad Holt didn't get to go to San Francisco. How he would have enjoyed the great fire of 1851!

In the meantime the *Eureka* had sailed down Lake Ontario and was reported on October 11 at French Creek, awaiting a tow boat to take her through the St. Lawrence canals. She reached Montreal on Wednesday, October 17, and cleared for Quebec the next day, reaching the latter port on Sunday, October 21.[20]

The appearance of the Cleveland vessel in Canadian waters called forth a learned and eloquent editorial on the part of the Montreal *Herald*,

[19] Further developments in the Holt case are followed in the *Daily True Democrat*, Sept. 25, Oct. 9, 24, 25, 26, 27, 29, 1849, the *Herald*, Oct. 24, 25, 26, 27, 29, and the *Plain Dealer*, Oct. 9, 29, and Dec. 31, 1849.

[20] *Plain Dealer*, Oct. 15, 1849; St. Catharines *Journal*, Oct. 11, 1849.

which was reproduced in the Quebec *Gazette*. Readers were reminded of the building of the *Griffon* by La Salle, the first sailing ship to navigate the inland waters above Niagara. Emphasis was put on the rapid growth of Cleveland to a city of twelve thousand or more inhabitants. And then attention was directed to the port to which the *Eureka* was bound, in California where Cabrillo and others in the service of Spain, with "all the eager avarice which prompted" their expeditions, "failed to discover the richest of all deposits of the precious metal." Due credit was given to the "civil engineer and his gigantic labours" for making it possible for vessels of such size to pass from the upper to the lower lakes and out to the sea. As to the voyage around the Horn, it was no longer, the editor declared, to be looked upon as a hardship. Besides, the *Eureka* was actually larger than most of the ships of the historic explorers such as Columbus, Magellan, Drake, or Cavendish. This voyage appeared to the *Herald* to be another notable landmark in the progress of civilization.[21]

While sightseeing in Montreal, Henry Howe left his cane, but managed to hunt it up before leaving town.

At Quebec several additional California emi-

[21] The Montreal *Herald* editorial is copied in the Quebec *Gazette*, Oct. 22, 1849.

grants came on board. Judge Joel Burnell of Charlotte, Chautauqua County, at the western extremity of New York state, was a frontier jurist, Methodist preacher, and farmer. He had eleven children, including six sons. One of these was Madison Burnell, for many years a leader in the Whig party in this region. Another was L. D. Burnell, previously mentioned, cobuilder and supercargo of the *Eureka*. A third was J. Ransom Burnell, a lawyer of Jamestown, the leading town of Chautauqua County. Ransom Burnell had joined his brother on the *Eureka*, and was one of those on board when the barque sailed from Cleveland.

Probably Ransom Burnell was instrumental in persuading another Chautauquan, "Professor" Llewellyn App Rogers, to follow his example. Rogers had attended the Jamestown schools and then entered Hamilton College, from which he graduated with the class of 1847. A daguerreotype taken in 1848 shows him as a round-faced, intelligent looking youngster in rather gaudy regalia, top hat, and bright vest. His nickname of "Professor" doubtless rose simply from the peculiarity of his having graduated from college. On October 19 he set out from Jamestown to join the expedition, traveling by way of Ogdensburg and Montreal and reaching Quebec on October 24, just the day before the scheduled sailing. Departure being delayed for three days, however, in order to complete repairs and finish taking on supplies, Rogers reported that he and Ransom Burnell were "furnished abundant leisure" for visiting "the numerous objects of interest in and adjacent to the 'city of fortifications.' "[22]

Twelve residents of Quebec signed up for passage. One was a law student, another a clerk, and a third a bartender. Seven belonged to the family of Garret Murphy, an innkeeper, and joined the Skears and the Bryans in the family cabin. The Murphy family included, besides the head of the house, his wife, four Murphy children, and Maria Malloy, a daughter of Mrs. Murphy by an earlier marriage. Maria Malloy and Ann Murphy, one of her half-sisters, were both about eighteen years of age and, according to an appreciative male eyewitness, "both amiable young women." It is clear enough that their coming on board considerably improved the prospects for a pleasant voyage.

After the *Eureka* was taken out of dry dock,

[22] *The Centennial History of Chautauqua County* (Jamestown, 1904), I, 200-201, and II, 348; Jamestown *Journal*, Oct. 19, 1849, and "L.A.R." (Llewellyn App Rogers) in the Jamestown *Journal*, March 22, 1850. Abbe includes Rogers in his passenger list and indicates that L. D. Burnell was the brother of J. Ransom and Madison Burnell. Information on Rogers obtained from an undated obituary in the Kane (Pennsylvania) *Republican* (Dec. 8, 1896) and from the Secretary of Hamilton College, citing the Hamilton College *Bulletin* of 1897, and Hamilton College, *Complete Alumni Register, 1812-1922* (Clinton, 1922).

her sheathing having been completed, more lumber loaded, and the supply of provisions replenished, including some oatmeal, salt fish, and hardtack, and Henry Howe having engineered another last-minute rescue of his errant walking stick, she weighed anchor on the afternoon of November 13, 1849. Three of the Quebec passengers were late in arriving at the pier. One caught a ride on a small steamboat and overtook the barque some ten miles downstream. Eleazer Abbe in his diary called it "almost maraculous good luck." The other two tardy passengers, William L. Ryan and W. Campbell, attempting to catch up in a row boat, had the decidedly bad luck of being left behind, having paid their two hundred dollars passage money each, watching the *Eureka* dwindle away on the horizon headed for California and carrying their luggage with her.

The *Quebec Mercury* gave the ship a fine editorial send-off. After noting that she was "the first vessel from the inland part of the United States which has proceeded to sea via Quebec," the *Eureka* was described as "by far the finest vessel which has sailed for California—her cabin is lofty and well ventilated." "Competent judges pronounce the vessel to be one of the strongest built ships in port, and prognosticate a speedy and safe voyage to the passengers, it being generally supposed that she will arrive at her destination 3 weeks or a month before those already started."[23]

At about the same time, November 13, 1849, two British ships, the *Panama* and the *Rory O'More,* also sailed from Quebec for California.[24]

[23] On the Murphys and the departure from Quebec, see the quotation from the Quebec *Mercury* in the *Plain Dealer,* Nov. 30, 1849, and the manuscript diary of Eleazer Abbe.

[24] Cleveland *Herald,* Nov. 23, 1849.

6.

Quebec to Rio

LATE in the short November afternoon the barque *Eureka* dropped down the St. Lawrence. The little boat containing the two tardy passengers fell hopelessly behind. The great rock and the citadel faded in the early twilight. All eyes now turned downstream where far beyond vision lay the Gulf and the open sea. More sail was shaken out and the ship heeled slightly as it was caught by a freshening breeze from the west.

The weather was fine, and "Professor" Rogers wrote appreciatively of the scenery in general and especially of the "beautiful white villas" which

studded the river bank all the way to Anacosti
Island, where the river widened into the bay. The
only snow they saw was that which glittered from
the summits of the Mountains of Ste Anne to the
south.

Five days out from Quebec, on Sunday afternoon, November 18, they passed between the island of St. Paul and Newfoundland into the Atlantic. Cape Breton Island was faintly visible to
the west as they swung southeast through the
mounting swells. The next morning this last sight
of land was gone. It was nearly four weeks before
they made their next landfall in the Cape Verde
Islands.[1]

And so they "sailed some time after leaving the
Gulf," as Dr. Baldwin wrote back to Cleveland,
"with fair winds, pleasant weather and joyful
hearts." But on Monday began a week of North
Atlantic storm during which they were "tossed
about most unmercifully, being unable to walk
or do anything in the cabin or any other part of
the vessel." The Jones boys agreed that it was
rather rough: "Everything was literally turned up-
side down. Every time the vessel made a lurch,
men, boys, tables, chairs, and spitoons were piled
over the floor on the lee side of the cabin in the
most beautiful confusion, while the gagging of the

[1] Llewellyn Rogers to "Frank," Rio de Janeiro, Jan. 20, 1850,
the Jamestown *Journal,* March 22, 1850.

poor sufferers in attempting to cast up, intermingling with the cries (made by the terrified ones) resounding from all parts of the cabin, made a most laughable, unintelligible jargon." The young physician agreed that "of all the evils which flesh is heir to none is so unpleasant at the time as sea sickness." Perhaps it was because he was not long experienced in dealing with this (or any other) illness that Baldwin despaired of the life of Robert Taylor, the Cleveland baker boy—or perhaps a baker has a naturally sensitive stomach. Anyway, Taylor was soon hale and hearty after they slipped, at the end of the week, into the warm and comparatively quiet Gulf Stream.[2]

After this introduction the Eurekans enjoyed fine weather, and most of them took a great interest in the strange and unfamiliar phenomena of deep sea travel. They noted the phosphorescence of the ship's wake at night, "glittering with innumerable and sparkling brilliants," and "were often not a little amused by whales rising to the surface of the water, blowing their noses and again disappearing." The Joneses thought the spouting of a whale sounded very much like a high-pressure steamboat. One bright afternoon, when they were in a calm, the captain allowed a small party of

[2] A. S. Baldwin's letter, "Bark Eureka, Jan. 3, 1850," *Plain Dealer*, March 12, 1850; and John and Henry Jones to Thomas Jones, Rio, January 20, 1850, Cleveland *Daily Herald*, March 13, 1850. The three succeeding paragraphs are from the same sources.

passengers to row ahead in a small boat and take a swim in the warm sea. "Hundreds of miles from land, immersed and floating in the mighty deep," Dr. Baldwin found it a "most poetic" experience. But a warning that there might be sharks about quickly brought the poetry to its last stanza.

"On Washing day," wrote John Jones, to his parents, "the deck presents a very laughable appearance, when every passenger may be seen trotting around with a wash bowl in one hand and a bundle of clothes in the other, perhaps a prototype of the diggings." "Dec. 13th," he reported, "we had a very fine heavy shower of rain, during which the sailors caught enough water for the passengers to do their washing with. Henry and I collected our dirty clothes together and washed them up with the neatness of any laundress, and with the despatch that would put the blush on a patent washing machine."

On December 15 the captain pointed out a dim shadow on the eastern horizon. It was San Antonio, one of the Cape Verde Islands, he said, some distance off Dakar on the west coast of Africa. The Ohioans must all have felt like Columbus in reverse as they forthwith proceeded to practice their newly acquired nautical vocabulary by shouting "Land Ho!" until they were hoarse. Then everybody began to smell pineapples, oranges, and bananas, proving, according to Baldwin, "that the knowledge of the near approach to land had a great effect on the olfactories, at least the imagination."

On Christmas Day the *Eureka* had reached 10° north latitude, and Jones marveled that the temperature was ninety in the shade "while you [in Cleveland] in all probability are even muffled up to keep your *noses* and *toeses* from freezing." After leaving the neighborhood of the Cape Verdes they had picked up the northeast trades and were now skimming along merrily toward the coast of South America.

With time hanging so heavily on their hands it was to be expected that the gold seekers would not miss the opportunity of participating in the traditional ceremony of crossing the line. Ransom Burnell described the event, which took place the day after Christmas, in a letter to friends back in Jamestown. The formalities began soon after sundown, when "NEPTUNE, trident in hand, his white flowing locks and venerable beard dripping with the dews of the ocean, attended by his train of satellites, scaled the bows of our barque, hailed the ship, seated himself in his chair of state, and ordered his officers to enforce the tribute due him." The "officers," supposedly persons who had crossed the line before, rounded up the landlubbers and initiated them into the ancient and honorable order of shellbacks, Neptune's loyal subjects.

Selected first to be inducted, probably because

of his reputation for testiness, was Henry Howe, the Cleveland carpenter. According to Burnell, he

resisted to the last, but to no purpose . . . . His god-ship put a few routine questions, and then informed him of the consequences of being caught where he had no business to be, without a bottle of the "O-be-joy-ful." Old "Pepper" [as Howe was nicknamed] not being able to liquidate, was seated on the 'barber's stool, most beautifully put through a coating of tar, soot and gum, scraped with the smooth side of an iron hoop, and then substantially drenched with a half dozen buckets of water.[3]

One after another in rapid succession, the others were treated in like fashion, and imme-diately became very efficient and enthusiastic in bringing in the remainder of the uninitiated. Some sought to escape by going up the rigging or by undressing and retiring to their berths, but all were brought before the throne and served alike. So "nearly every pair of whiskers (and they were by no means few)" was ruined before the sick and irascible Captain Monroe burst out on deck to bring the proceedings to an end. "Here," con-cluded Burnell, "the 'crittur' passed rapidly once or twice around, being embraced very affection-ately, and we closed the business after enjoying more real fun than was ever crowded into one short evening, and more than I ever dreamed could be had in a trip to California by way of the Horn."

[3] Excerpt of a letter from "friend B ***" [Ransom Burnell] printed in the Jamestown *Journal*, March 22, 1850.

As was usual on the gold ships, there was a great deal of complaint about the provisions. Eleazer Abbe of Elyria wrote in his diary that there was much "Cusing and Daming Mr. Adair for not better furnish[ing] the ship." "Old Pepper" Howe was particularly bitter. "I wish it to be distinctly understood," he wrote back to Cleveland, "that we have for our provisions, bad butter, that in most cases was not fit for soap grease; corned beef, third quality, or stinking mackerel, freshened with salt water; potatoes, what few we did have, that were condemned in Quebec as unfit for cattle feed, and we were at least three weeks out before we could even get dry beans cooked in any shape." He let it be doubly clear that he intended to sue the owners as soon as the opportunity presented itself. To meet this criticism in part, young Beardsley was dismissed from his position as steward and another member of the crew took his place.[4]

In the meantime they were approaching South America. When Cape Frio loomed up hazily to the southwest, all eyes were strained to identify the other famous landmarks of the Brazilian coast. The former landlubbers, all now being shellbacks, felt fully qualified to assist the officers and crew, in whom they seem to have had little confidence anyway. Abbe gives some sense of the curiosity and suspense which prevailed:

[4] Henry Howe to "Friend Schwab," "Barque 'Eureka' Jan. 16, 1850, in Bay of Rio Jainero," *Plain Dealer*, March 12, 1850.

When we got in sight of Rio many got considerably
excited on account of no one knowing which was
shugar loaf Rock and Some betting took place as
many Peaks and Rocks stood out in view and no one
on bord appeared to now which was the wone, it
being near night and the Officers not feeling it safe
to run into port that night of the 8th of Jan. 1850
we stood out untill the next morning and it being
something of a calm did not get in until near noon
of the 9th of Jan. 1850 when we passed the fort and
let go the anchor about three Miles From Shore.[5]

So, fifty-seven days out of **Quebec**, the *Eureka*
sailed past Sugar Loaf, the Corcovado, Two Brothers Island, and the Moro del Castello guarding the
entrance, and came to rest in the magnificent bay
of the River of January. "Professor" Rogers, who
seems to have been particularly sensitive to romantic scenery, was greatly impressed with the fine,
land-locked harbor "studded with islands crowned
with forts, convents, castellated parapets, and picturesque ruins."[6]

The country and small town boys from Ohio,
New York, and Michigan, who had never, until
they visited Montreal and Quebec, seen a community larger than the frontier towns of Cleveland and Detroit, had their eyes opened by this
great metropolis of South America. The port
authorities let no one go ashore the first night, but
the myriad twinkling gaslights, which appeared in

[5] MS diary of Eleazer Abbe.
[6] Llewellyn Rogers in the Jamestown *Journal*, March 22, 1850.

the evening, extending for miles along the shore and up into the hills, gave them some hint of what to expect.

On Thursday, January 10, the small boats were busy ferrying passengers and crew to the city, where they were landed at the stairs leading up to the Palace Square. Here, immediately, they were confronted with the leading public house—the Hotel Pharoux—the imperial palace, and a variety of convents and chapels. Here they were thrust directly into the hurly-burly of city traffic: horse- and mule-drawn carriages dashing recklessly over the pavements; gangs of barefooted African slaves trotting by with great sacks of coffee on their heads; others hauling carts filled with boxes and bales to and from the waterside; policemen, uniformed like soldiers, loitering on the corners and near the fountain; and well-dressed merchants going to the exchange.

John Jones spent his first evening at the Royal Opera. He made no mention of the nature of the performance in his letter home, but he reported that the opera house was "a splendid building capable of accomodating 3 or 4000 persons" with "200 private boxes besides the apartment set apart for the royal family, which is furnished off in most gorgeous style." Like most Americans he was greatly thrilled by the sight of a real reigning monarch.

I had the plasure of seeing the Emperor, Empress and suite at the performance, and I must say that I consider him a very superior looking man. The Empress is quite a plain looking woman, apparently 8 or 10 years older than her husband. They were conveyed to and from the opera in a splendid barouche drawn by six mules, followed by a great number of foot and horse guard.[7]

It seems odd that the Emperor should have attended the opera at this time, for on the preceding day, the very day that the *Eureka* entered the bay, his only living son and heir to the throne had died when not yet quite a year and a half old. Probably most of the Eurekans witnessed the great state funeral on the following Saturday. According to young Jones: "The thundering of the cannon from all the Batteries and also from three Brazilian Men of War were kept up all day long, which together with the continued roar of the artillery, made the greatest *Hullabaloo* I ever saw kicked up. In the evening there was the greatest torch light procession I ever witnessed; it was entirely composed of cavalry and infantry; they marched and counter marched to the Palace Square to the most doleful music till about 12 o'clock." Emperor Dom Pedro was, of course, dressed in mourning, in a black suit and frock coat, black cravat and

[7] John and Henry Jones in the Cleveland *Daily Herald*, March 13, 1850.

tall silk hat, and on his breast the blazing diamonds
of the Imperial Order of the Southern Cross.[8]

Jones was disdainful of the Brazilian soldiers,
who, he thought, "presented a most laughable appearance," "a motley looking crowd," being of all
shades from blackest Africans to pure Portuguese.
Individual soldiers, he declared, would often
leave the ranks to go into a shop to get a drink
of liquor or a cigar. "One hundred Yankees [of
course] could put a thousand of them to flight."
He found the people in general "perfectly inoffen-
sive" but "lazy and inefficient and at least two
centuries behind the Americans, i.e., the Yankees."

All were ecstatic in their descriptions of the
rich verdure and the wealth of tropical fruits. It
was a great luxury to be able to eat fresh fruit
after the long weeks at sea on salt beef and hard
tack. Dr. Baldwin reveled in the "oranges, lemons,
cocoa nuts, pine apples, coffee, bananas, bread
fruit." He was particularly interested in the pineapples, which, he wrote to his Ohio friends, grow
"somewhat similar to the cabbage in the States,
but being surrounded by a much narrower leaf."[9]

[8] Mary W. Williams, *Dom Pedro the Magnanimous, Second
Emperor of Brazil* (Chapel Hill, 1937) , pp. 89-90 and 92.

[9] Letter from A. S. Baldwin, Rio de Janeiro, Jan. 18 and 20,
1850, Cleveland *Plain Dealer*, March 13, 1850. There is excellent
background material on Rio at the time in D. P. Kidder and
J. C. Fletcher, *Brazil and the Brazilians, Portrayed in Historical
and Descriptive Sketches* (Philadelphia and Columbus, 1857) .
Much of the material in this work seems to have been drawn
from Charles Wilkes, *Narrative of the United States Exploring
Expedition during the Years, 1838, 1839, 1840, 1841, 1842* (5
vols.; Philadelphia, 1950).

"Old Pepper" Howe stopped to buy some oranges in an establishment "of such a jaw-breaking name that I could not read it twice alike," laid down his precious cane, and lost it for good.[10]

Llewellyn Rogers was overwhelmed by the luxuriance of the gardens in the city's suburbs, "laid out with good taste, furnishing every variety of native plants, flowers of exquisite beauty, and all the rich and rare fruits peculiar to the tropics." The *Passeio Publico,* a sort of metropolitan park, provided with fountains, shaded paths, and a great variety of blooming plants and picturesque trees and shrubs, all illuminated in the evening, was a mecca for all visitors. It was somewhat elevated and furnished an impressive view of the city, Sugar Loaf, and the ocean beyond. Here, according to Rogers, strangers could "go with impunity, and pluck any specimens they choose." The Imperial Botanical Gardens, some miles from the city in the interior, made an even more favorable impression.

To John Jones the climate seemed "perfectly delightful . . . no sudden changes, but the same agreeable temperature all the year long." Indeed, he declared, it would be the finest place to live "on the face of Gods Green Earth . . . —if it was only a free country owned and inhabited by free *white men.*"

[10] Howe's letter from Rio dated Jan. 16, 1850, published in the Cleveland *Plain Dealer,* March 12, 1850.

The "Professor" found "the white portion of the inhabitants . . . very polite, fond of excitement and amusements," and interested in the fine arts. He noted that there were theatrical performances nightly and bullfights every week. Dr. Baldwin was surprised to discover that Sunday was the great day for recreation. All bullfights were on Sunday, and the famous feather-flowers and other exhibits in the national museum could be seen only on that day.[11]

The Gold Rush had brought more of the outside world to Rio than it had ever seen before. M. Pharoux, proprietor of the chief waterfront hotel, told Jones that he had entertained some thirty thousand goldseekers at his establishment already, and that he had seen as many as fifty California-bound vessels in the harbor at one time. Jones himself noted twenty-five different gold ships in the bay during the two weeks of the *Eureka's* stay. He estimated that each of them carried from fifty to a hundred passengers.[12] The *Rory O'More,* which had left Quebec the same time as the *Eureka,* was at Rio when the barque arrived, having made the trip twelve days faster. A week after the *Eureka* had come to anchor, three gold ships from Boston came in on the same

[11] Rogers' letter of Jan. 20, 1850 and Baldwin's letters of Jan. 18 and 20, 1850, cited above.
[12] John and Henry Jones's letter of Jan. 20, 1850, cited above.

day: the brig *Triumph* (which had sprung her mainmast and lost a man off the rigging in a storm), the barque *Helen S. Page,* and the barque *Orion* of Falmouth. On the nineteenth the ship *Euphrasia,* five hundred tons, of Newburyport, Massachusetts, joined the considerable fleet already in the bay and her passengers went ashore to see the strange sights and enjoy the exotic fruits of Brazil's leading city. Besides the many sailing ships, the Ohioans noted two steamers, the *Sarah Sands* and the *Tennessee,* the latter having made it from New York in the record time of twenty-four days.[13]

At this time David Tod, prominent politician and businessman of Youngstown and candidate for governor of Ohio in 1844, was the American minister to Brazil. He made a special point of inviting his neighbors from the Western Reserve to call on him. John Jones, who had letters of introduction to him from a mutual acquaintance, was greatly pleased by the hearty cordiality with which the minister welcomed him. Tod seems to

[13] On the *Euphrasia* and the *Orion* and other ships at Rio the author has used Thomas Sherman's MS "Log Book" of the voyage of the *Euphrasia,* a copy of which is in the Essex Institute Library at Salem; parts of the original log book of the *Orion* in the library of the California Historical Society in San Francisco; and Seth Draper, *Voyage of the Bark Orion from Boston around Cape Horn to San Francisco, Cal., in the Year 1849, Touching at Rio de Janeiro and Juan Fernandez* (Providence, 1870). The registration of the *Euphrasia* is given in "Ship Registers of the District of Newburyport, 1789-1870," Essex Institute, *Historical Collections,* LXX (July, 1934), 311.

have given his guest quite a lecture on Brazil and the Brazilians.

The consul at Rio was the former governor, Edward Kent of Maine, a new Whig appointee. It was the special task of the consul to straighten out the often-tangled affairs of visiting American ships. The *Euphrasia* had a tremendous ruckus over food. A gold-seeker from the *Orion* reported that the skipper of the *Euphrasia* got a "regular overhauling from the passengers as soon as he landed." He added: "I saw him cry like a child." The consul got the captain to promise better fare for the remainder of the voyage.

There was a similar squabble among the Eurekans. The passengers were discontented, the crew was rebellious, the captain was sick, the first mate seems to have been brutal and insubordinate. L. D. Burnell, the supercargo, as part owner of the ship and representative of the other owner, considered himself superior in authority to the captain. Burnell and Freeman, the first mate, led one faction, including a small group of passengers. Captain Monroe, the second mate, and most of the passengers and crew stood together against this clique. Many of the crew refused to take orders from the first mate; the captain had been partly incapacitated for some time and was often unable to carry out his duties. When the vessel was in port he was absent on shore most of the time.

Things went from bad to awful. "Old Pepper" Howe said, "We are all dirty, ragged, hungry and saucy and the smartest man is the best fellow." Noisy disputes were the order of the day. Some of those returning from visits to the city had stayed too long in the grog shops. Fights broke out at all hours of the day and night. W. W. Culver, the Green Creek lawyer, and Freeman, the first mate, committed an assault upon the person of Edward Beardsley, who had formerly been the steward, which resulted in the breaking of several bones in Beardsley's ankle. Much of the time nobody was on board who could exercise any authority. Very little, if any, progress was made at first in revictualing and providing fresh water.

A row was soon kicked up, [wrote Eleazer Abbe in his diary] and noise and confusion reigned through fore and aft. Some were for Monroe our Capt and some for L D B and the mate and the contest raged for 2 or 3 days with considerable wind and some showed fight until a committy was appointed to wait on Capt Monroe and ascertain whether he could and would vitual the Ship and also whether he wished to go on any further as Commander.

Monroe had refused to submit to the ministrations of young Dr. Baldwin. He now visited various physicians in Rio, and they advised him that his illness was mortal, perhaps tuberculosis, and he should return home if he ever wished to see it again. Under these circumstances Consul Kent

acted, appointing a new captain by the name of McQueen.

McQueen and Burnell seemed to get along well enough. On January 22, numerous scuttlebutts of fresh water and kegs of biscuit and salt beef were got on board, and all preparations rapidly made for departure on the next leg of the journey.[14]

So all together within a few hours of each other the *Triumph,* with her mainmast repaired, the *Orion,* the *Helen S. Page,* the ship *Euphrasia* of Newburyport, and the barque *Eureka* of Cleveland, Captain McQueen commanding, sailed out of Rio and headed south.

[14] These paragraphs are based upon the Abbe diary and the letters of the Jones boys and Henry Howe cited above.

7.

'Round the Horn

EDWARD BEARDSLEY, the deposed steward, was agonizing in his berth as the crew tugged on the windlass and, with a final shout, brought up the dripping anchor. They were answered with three cheers from the brig *Panama,* which had sailed with them from Quebec. As the *Panama* held to her moorings, the *Eureka* stood out to sea, but at dusk the barque was becalmed still in sight of the now familiar Sugar Loaf.

Beardsley was suffering from a badly broken ankle, the result of the brutal assault by the drunken mate two days before. He also com-

plained of a severe headache and pain in his back
and was running a high temperature. When Dr.
Baldwin recognized these symptoms of the dreaded
yellow fever the general good humor and high
spirits incident to sailing gave way to depression
and near panic. Many of the passengers made
their beds in the cordage or the longboat on the
open deck for fear of infection. As a result of
the exposure thus incurred Eleazer Abbe caught a
cold, had a "Dizzy Sort of a head," and noted in his
diary that he took two pills, the first time he had
resorted to his private medical supply.

Halsey Doan, the two Jones boys, and another
young bachelor volunteered to care for the ailing
Beardsley. Perhaps Doan felt that his experience
with cholera in Sandusky would help him in dealing with this other mortal pestilence. Henry
Jones's berth was curtained off to make a stuffy
little sick room, as much for the supposed protec-
tion of the other voyagers as out of consideration
for the patient.

By the afternoon of the second day out, a
breeze had picked up, the ship was rolling in a
choppy sea, and Sugar Loaf had faded on the horizon. Beardsley was much worse; he was apparently
in excruciating pain and his skin was turning a
bright golden yellow. The air of his little chamber
became so fetid that his nurses took turns in staying

with him a few minutes at a time. Late in the evening he died.

John Jones and Henry Howe sewed up the corpse in the bed clothes, including Henry Jones's mattress. (Perhaps Howe was selected for this task because he was a carpenter, and on land carpenters made coffins.) Tradition prescribed that the last stitch should be taken through the nose. About an hour after death the "burial" took place. The ship hove to, and all passengers and crew gathered near the lee rail where the body in its bulky shroud was laid on a board. Heads were uncovered. Captain Burnell, the supercargo, read the prayer. As he repeated the words, "we therefore commit this body to the deep," the board was tipped up. With a hollow *ulck* the remains of Edward Beardsley, formerly of 17 Mandrake Lane, Cleveland, slipped into the sea.

Orlando Cutter noted the eerie moonlight. John Jones wrote that "The night was dark, and the wind as it whistled through the rigging, never sounded so mournfully." But, moonlit or dark, the scene made a great impression on all who were present, as each wondered whether he might be the next victim. "As for myself," Eleazer Abbe wrote in his diary, "I am considerable indisposed owing in part to Mr. Beardsley's death by Yellow Fever which considerably excited my mind."

For some time the cabin underwent disinfec-

tion by burnt tar and brimstone, the most power-
ful smells being considered most effective for such
purposes. Beardsley's gold watch was sent back
to his widow in Cleveland, and Henry Jones
learned to sleep sound without a mattress. Abbe
found the "Passengers more peacible and more
thoughtful than usual."

It was Beardsley's tragic misfortune that the
voyage was not hastened by a few weeks. Apparently no one on board the *Eureka* knew at the time
that the first case of yellow fever in the history of
Rio de Janeiro had developed less than a month
before. If the Eurekans had visited the city only
three or four weeks earlier no poisonous mosquito
would have awaited them.

A few days later a German sailor died of the
same disease, and was likewise buried at sea. Abbe
sprained his rhetoric in an effort to give an adequate description of the event: "He was soon taken
from the Forecastle and the usual Funeral Services
Performed And before Dark he the sick sailor . . .
Was consined to his waterry Grave in the Deep
Waters to become food for the Sharks of the Broad
Atlantic—as one was seen a short time before
Lurking about the Ship." There were no other
cases of yellow fever, and soon thoughts and con-
versation turned to other interests and other fears.[1]

[1] On Beardsley's death the sources, besides the Abbe diary,
are John and Henry Jones to parents, Valparaiso, Chile, March
15, 1850, printed in the *Plain Dealer*, June 24, 1850; Henry

But at least one shark was still hungry the next day—hungry enough to take the bait and be caught and hauled on board. "I helped skin him," bragged John Jones, "and have preserved one of his teeth and fins, and eat a slice of his body." According to both Abbe and Cutter this monster of the sea was eight feet long.

A sport that helped to pass many long hours was harpooning porpoises, vast schools of which leaped alongside the ship in the waters between Rio and Cape Horn. Orlando Cutter wrote home to his father, the Cleveland auctioneer:

On Friday February 15th quite an amusing incident occurred . . . . One of our passengers went out on the martingale stays [spars under the bowsprit near the water line] to harpoon porpoises, and while there the vessel's course was changed, which caused her to dip heavily in a heavy sea which was running, and twice he was completely under water, and the second time he went down he could not be seen and it was feared he was washed off, but when the vessel rose on the next wave, he was clinging to the rope looking like a drowned rat, having got a good ducking and lost his hat.

Shooting at targets, at gulls and other birds, was another popular diversion. William Stacey

Howe to his father, Valparaiso, March 14, 1850, *Plain Dealer*, June 22, 1850; and Orlando Cutter's letter of March 15, 1850, in the *Daily Herald*, June 24, 1850. For the custom of burial at sea, see Leland P. Lovette, *Naval Customs, Traditions and Usage* (Annapolis, 1939), pp. 38-42. There is a useful account of yellow fever in Brazil in Kidder and Fletcher, *Brazil and the Brazilians*, pp. 599-603.

of Blissfield, Michigan, was the leading marksman;
Abbe called him "Our celebrated Gaimster." On
February 10, in Latitude 43° 28′, Eleazer Abbe recorded: "A large sea fowl was shot today cald Albert Ross it was about the size of a wild goose and
looks some like one." From then on "Albert Ross"
was much in evidence. While making the passage
of the cape Stacey shot two albatross, one on the
19th and another on Washington's Birthday. On
the first occasion the *Eureka* was in a calm, so the
captain allowed a boat to be lowered to retrieve
the bird. It was found to weigh about fifteen
pounds and had a wing stretch of eight to ten feet.

On the last day of January they had run into a
heavy gale, "which caused our bark [to] groan and
toss about," wrote Abbe, "as though she would fall
to pieces, but she held up remarkably well and no
accident happened, except tumbling and nocking
about the cabbin of Both Passengers and chairs and
as the setting tables was dispensed with every one
had to walk up to the Stand and help himself to
tea & grub and such a looking mess or motley crew
I never saw before." But everyone had recognized
that such a storm as this was only a slight foretaste
of what they could expect at the Horn.

The rounding of the Cape was the crisis of the
voyage. After leaving Rio there was much speculation about this notorious passage, and the progress of the vessel toward the south was measured

by degree with a growing sense of excitement.
The 24th parallel of south latitude was passed on
January 26, three days out. On the 31st day of the
month they crossed the 31st parallel. Twelve degrees more, as we have noted, had been added by
the tenth of February when the first "Albert Ross"
was shot. At night an unfamiilar sky opened to
the view of the North Americans. The Great
Bear had long since dropped out of sight, and the
Cross of the South hung high. By Sunday, February 17, the word got around that they must be
in the neighborhood of Staten Land, the Straits of
Le Maire, and Tierra del Fuego. Abbe wrote in
his diary:

This is the fourth Lords Day sence we Left Rio. Our
Gallant Bark ceeps her course with a smart Breese and
a heavy fogg with some rain in the morning. The
fog and clouds continued throughout the day so that
no Latitude nor Longitude was taken . . . . Blowed to
almost a gale . . . until about 11 o'clock at night.
Then the Elephant began to show when a perfect
Gale Hove up from the west & S W and the cabin
was soon in confusion and some of the Passengers got
up and did no more go to bed for fear through the
balance of the night when the mountain billows
Rooled and tumbled the Bark most furiously.

All the day following the wind and the waves piled
out of the west as the jealous elements hurled the
Eureka back into the Atlantic. It was clear enough
to the veriest landlubber of a ship full of Mid-

western landlubbers that they had opened the door
to the famous passage 'round Cape Horn. The
announcement that the 55th parallel had been
passed was anticlimactic.

The next day, February 19, was so quiet that
the captain permitted the passengers to get out a
boat to recover Stacey's second albatross. But the
twentieth, as Orlando Cutter reported in a letter
back to Cleveland,

> . . . came in with a perfect gush of a gale . . . . The
> wind blew a regular hurricane, and all our light sails
> were furled, and the top-sails close reefed. In at-
> tempting to reef the fore-sail it was torn to tatters
> and rendered unfit for use . . . . But as the wind came
> from the northeast quarter and our course was south-
> west, we were scudding before it at the rate of 8 to
> 10 knots per hour with nothing but close reefed top-
> sails set, and the waves came rolling on after us like
> young mountains . . . . But onward sped our gallant
> craft and heeded them not.

The young auctioneer, the marble cutter's son,
and the Elyria farmer all became poetic in extoll-
ing the staunchness and seaworthiness of the
barque *Eureka* from Black River, Lorain County,
Ohio, as she beat around the southernmost tip of
the American continent.

It took about two weeks to make it into the
Pacific, days of damp, cold, biting wind, even
though it was the southern summer, days of alter-
nating calm and furious storm. Sometimes during

the fierce blows two men were kept at the wheel with two others standing by to relieve them. Solemn thoughts came to many; for Abbe it was a religious experience. He recognized the pervasive "influence of the Angry God of the Ocean which tumbles the mighty deep into such awful commotion," and he gave thanks to "the Great God our Creator" for the lesson learned by "the appearing of the tumbling blue waters."

During much of the time, Abbe was "considerably indisposed" as a result of the cold, the dampness, homesickness, and the constant plunging of the ship. He was a little more comfortable after a stove was put up in the cabin on the twenty-sixth. Even then he was not too happy, because all the others crowded into the cabin around the stove, where they sat all day long during the storm under the dim and violently swinging lamp, singing, laughing, and whittling. He complained that many, the boys particularly, were "vary unjentelmanly." With so many crowded into such close quarters with nothing much to do, there were undoubtedly many loud and angry altercations. Just a week before, the captain had had to threaten to put one of the passengers in irons for swearing and making too much noise. It did not help either that much of the time the wind blew down through the smoke pipe and filled the whole place with acrid, choking smoke, bringing on much coughing and sneezing.

As escape from the elements was sought in the cabin so, whenever the storm relented, most men found relief from the cramped quarters and the close, smokey air of the cabin on the open deck. The weather improved enough on the afternoon of the twenty-second of February so that, as Abbe stated it, "a little merriment was had by the Passengers in celebrating the Berth Day of the beloved Father of our country Gen. George Washington." Voyagers to California seldom missed the opportunity to celebrate a holiday, especially a patriotic one. It was clear enough to them that the nation which had just acquired gold-rich California was well on the way to a glorious destiny.

At this stage of the journey other ships were usually in sight, and they were always objects of much interest and speculation. The whaler *Clementine* of Bremen, full of oil and headed back to her home port, must have been kept busy hailing California-bound ships. On February 20 she spoke the barque *Orion,* one of whose passengers painted a word picture of her as she sailed close reefed, through the heavy Cape Horn sea "at one moment riding high on the top of some huge wave and rolling till the glittering copper on her bottom could be seen almost to her keel, and the next moment plunging down into the sea until nothing

could be seen but her naked topmasts."[2]   (Such a
description helps the reader to understand why
food was not a matter of so much interest during
this part of the voyage.)   On the next day, February
21, the *Clementine* hailed the *Eureka* and reported
the meeting with her sister gold ship.

On the evening of February 24 five sails were
visible at one time, all seemingly drawn by the
magnet of the diggings on the American River.
These vessels were not identified but the *Euphrasia*
or the *Orion* might have been among them.   Occasionally the Eurekans engaged in what were
largely imaginary races with other California-
bound ships.   Cutter reported proudly on one of
these affairs: "The next morning the wind shifted,
so that we were running square before it, and the
wind growing more strong, by 12 o'clock we over-
hauled and passed her, and at dark she was nearly
out of sight astern."   Many coins and jack-knives
must have changed hands in settling the bets on
this contest.

By the first of March they were well into the
Pacific.   The ship kept a fairly even keel for the
first time since they had passed Staten Land, and
the planks under the passengers' feet had "that
Spirit Stiring onward motion," that "exhilerating
and darting spring" which had been so much
missed in the preceding fortnight.   Eleazer Abbe

[2] Draper, *Voyage of the Bark Orion,* pp. 51-52.

"took some phisic," his dizziness cleared up, and his health generally improved. Now they bowled along toward the north again. On March 3 they were back at the 52nd parallel; within a week they were at the 40th. And now they began looking forward to the next landing. As a steady fresh breeze blew up from the southeast the "Prospect began to briten with the . . . Anticipation of Steping again on tereferma in the Emporian Citty of Valparaiso."

But Elyria, Cleveland, Milan, Jamestown, Painesville seemed farther away than ever, and homesickness had a way of returning again with a renewed and heart-sickening force even on these more propitious days of the journey. To farmer Abbe "every loud blast" was "burdened with anxious fears" as the ship plowed "through the foaming billows." And even now, when they were well past the fearful seas off Cape Horn, his thoughts often turned longingly to his "loved Wife and Children and Parents, brothers and sisters at home." Did not Betsey and the five little children sometimes awaken in the stormy night and "commend his ceeping to one Whome the Winds and the sea Obey?" Other passengers were less sentimental or failed at least to record their moods for us.

A variety of methods of killing time was utilized. Stacey had some more sport with albatross.

Many an hour was passed by little groups sitting around in the lee of a coil of rope or in the longboat griping about the food. Then you could always get up a searching party to look for Benizer's money. After all, they were goldhunters, and if there was gold to be found right on the ship why not begin now?

J. S. Benizer, who listed his occupation as that of tailor, came from near Wooster in Wayne County, Ohio. He apparently had taken seriously the warning often repeated in the newspapers that a certain amount of capital was needed for those who would start life over again in the gold fields, for he carried with him in his trunk some two hundred and seventy dollars in gold pieces.

While the *Eureka* was lying at anchor in the bay at Rio de Janeiro his trunk was ransacked and the gold taken. The vessel was immediately searched, but neither gold nor evidence of the identity of the thief was found. Here was a major mystery. It is unlikely that there was a single person on board, not excluding the thief, who did not at one time or another advance a solution or point the finger of suspicion at some unpopular or unfriendly individual. Some insisted that the owners of the vessel, under the law as it applied to common carriers, were responsible for all losses sustained by passengers, and therefore Adair and Burnell would have to compensate Benizer. The two "Legal Gentleman" attracted considerable attention by their learned arguments on the matter. Doubtless Ranson Burnell sustained the interests of his brother. Logic would suggest that the other lawyer, W. W. Culver of Green Creek, Ohio, would have been likely to take the other side. Halsey Doan was only a law student and may not, therefore, have felt that he was in any position to speak with authority.

On March 5, ten days before arrival at Valparaiso, a special committee was appointed to make another and more thorough search for the gold. The effort was continued through two days, but nothing was discovered, if one excepts an old pair of boots found under some sacks of salt in the hold. As no one claimed these boots, they were raffled off, and the winner of the raffle sold them at auction for 62½ cents to Schuyler Strong, the former butcher from Elyria. The matter of Benizer's gold pieces remained a mystery.[3]

In general, it seems to have been the consensus among the passengers that Adair, Burnell, the steward, or *somebody* was cheating them out of their promised provisions. The diet was sufficiently monotonous and probably often poorly

[3] On Benizer and his gold, see letter from Deacon in the *Plain Dealer,* June 7, 1851, quoting a San Francisco paper, and Abbe's diary for Feb. 3 and March 5 and 6, 1850. The Wooster *Democrat,* Oct. 4, 1849, notes that "J. S. Brenizer," a passenger on the *Eureka,* gave his address as Wayne County. The editor apparently had never heard of him before.

prepared and served. The chances are, however, that they would have complained about it anyway.

During the long wait at Rio conditions were unusually bad, partly because of the frequent absence ashore of the cooks and the steward. It was all very disorderly according to Abbe: "One table has been neglected being set and such a crabble as took place when the Bell rang for our Meals is most ridiculous—swearing and cursing about living on Hard tack & Horse Beef . . . . I for one never fared so hard & so miserally entertained in the shape of Ship Cabbin fare nor do I ever again wish to see or experience the like." After leaving port, the passengers fared better. For breakfast the first day out they were served cold biscuit, cold beef, fried pork, fried mush, and potatoes with onions. The dessert at noon was "Plumb Pudden"—there was no grumbling. Unfortunately, soon afterward the sea became rough, and most people lost both breakfast and dinner over the rail.

Three days later Abbe could still declare that there was no complaint about the victuals; plum pudding was again served for dinner. At the end of a week the diet had settled down to hard tack, salt pork, and beef, but on the thirtieth of January there was a "General Call for Cakes and Duff." This last item seems to have been plum pudding without the plums, or something of that sort. Not much attention was given to food on the passage of the Horn, but on March 6 there was "some excitement on account of the badness of the pea soup." Perhaps this pea soup, as well as the general filthiness of the cabin, had something to do with the appointment of a third steward two days later.

At the ports the passengers were able to bring some pressure to bear to secure better accommodations, and the last night out before landing at Valparaiso there was more complaining, apparently, than at any time since they had left Rio. The Abbe diary contains a rather detailed description of the caucus:

Our supper was that poor and crusty that . . . through the evening little groups were Huddled together discussing the question of making a general rush at this Port for better living and about Ten Oclock in the Evening and directly in front of my berth a general collecttion of the big guns was collectted throughing out their Anathamy on the officers and Proprietors and L. D. Burnell and the Counsellor Burnell with now and then a heavy Oath which after about an hour discussion broke up with a Sharpe Rebuke from Doct Baldwin on George Hickox for being so forward in all such matter he being a minor . . . . I had turned in early and was annoyd not being able to get to Sleep.

George Hickox seems to have been a rather aggressive youngster.

After a voyage of fifty days, punctuated by the yellow fever scare, the killing of sharks, porpoises, and albatross, the terrifying storms of the Cape, and periodic hunts for Benizer's gold pieces, the freshwater barque *Eureka* came to anchor in the broad bay off Valparaiso. On March 15 in this "vale of paradise" the gold-hunters again delightedly set foot on what Abbe called "tery fermy" or "tereferma."

8.

To the Golden Gate

THE *Eureka* came to anchor about two and a half miles off the city of Valparaiso on the evening of March 14, 1850. Early the following morning a small boat came alongside with a very welcome supply of fresh fruit: apples, pears, peaches, and grapes.

A few passengers went ashore in the fruit boat. Others proposed to row in in the ship's tender. Mr. Freeman, the truculent first mate, forbade it; but, as soon at he was out of sight, they took the boat anyway and made for the city. Upon landing, they reported their action to Captain McQueen, who made no objection, indicating something of the status of the mate. They made the rounds of the markets, buying many of the excellent and cheap fruits and sweet potatoes. Orlando Cutter, who had a professional interest in street sales, declared them to be of superlative quality. John Jones agreed. "I have seen some of the finest peaches and apples, since coming here, I ever saw in my life," he wrote to his parents. "You can go to a stall in any of the fruit markets and eat all the apricots, peaches, nectarines, figs, grapes of every description, for a sixpence."[1]

Jones found the city a "mean looking place," but other voyagers preferred it to Rio. "I cannot enter into a description of the city," he continued, "not having sufficient time. Suffice it to say, I have visited everything worthy of note about it. Their olive groves, their graveyards and its beautiful sculpturings [this would interest Father Jones], their churches and their public buildings." He promised, when he got home, to spend several long evenings in telling about them. He didn't realize how long it would be before he would visit Cleveland again.

The alcoholic beverages available ashore had more attractions for some of the emigrants than

[1] John and Henry Jones to parents, Valparaiso, March 19, 1850, Cleveland *Plain Dealer,* June 24, 1850; Orlando Cutter, Jr., to his brother, Valparaiso, March 15, 1850, Cleveland *Daily Herald,* June 24, 1850; and entries in the MS diary of Eleazer Abbe. The diary is the chief source for this chapter.

any fruit, no matter how cheap or perfect. Abbe wrote in his diary that "the influence of lickare . . . often Created a row on bord of the celebrated bark Eureka." One night, when one or two came on board "prety well cornd," lawyer Culver engaged in a set-to with O. H. Russell, the Quebec bartender. On another occasion the diarist reported that some of the passengers and crew were "beastly drunk." He feared that they would "make a poor chance of it in the diggings" if they were not more temperate. Again he reported "a common Drunken Frollick" which caused "a most heidous noise." He was disappointed to note that the second mate was involved in this latter affray.

A good deal of time was passed tramping about the town and environs and rowing around the bay. One day Freeman Eggleston of Independence, Ohio; George B. Harvey, ship carpenter; Robert Taylor, baker; and Eleazer Abbe rowed to the east side of the bay and were caught by a storm. A heavy sea began to roll in and it was "with much toil, hazard and difficulty" that they were able to get back to the ship. There was always a good deal of fishing going on; one man caught "a singular looking Fish . . . having ten horns with a head that slid out and in like a turtle." It sounds like one of the beasts of the Apocalypse.

Sunday, March 23, 1850, was Easter. This caused the diarist to turn his "thoughts with great wonder and admiration back to that glorious first Day when Christ Our Master and Saviour Rose triumphant from the Grave." He went ashore and "attended meeting at catholic church, saw their forms and ceremonies but could not understand a word of their preaching."

Three or four vessels arrived from California in search of supplies, and the outbound goldseekers avidly absorbed all the information they could get from their crews about conditions in San Francisco and the gold mines. Abbe and some other Eurekans "went on bord the Ship *Sweden* lately from California where they Showed us specimens of Gold dust just as they dug it, in its native State both of the course and the fine and they informed us the way and manner of diging, and also the uncertainty of health which created something of an excitement on bord."

There was a good deal of social intercourse with the passengers of the ship *Euphrasia* of Newburyport, "a jolly set numbering one hundred and forty nine." Some rivalry was developed as to which, the *Eureka* or the *Euphrasia,* would reach San Francisco first. George B. Harvey, one of the carpenters from Cleveland, found that some of the men on the latter vessel were acquainted with relatives of his in Maine and Massachusetts. It's a small world, don't you know?

Mr. Freeman appeared before the United States consul and preferred charges against Orlando Cutter for interfering in an argument between the mate and one of the crew. These charges were dismissed after a hearing. Later on, however, the consul dismissed the mate, and Mr. Freeman went ahead to California on another ship. To most of those on board it was good riddance. John Jones called Freeman "as vain and tyrannical a man as ever I saw."[2]

Burnell had to mortgage the ship at a heavy discount in order to pay for needed supplies, and the negotiation of this loan somewhat delayed the departure. Some passengers also procured supplemental provisions for their own personal use. Eleazer Abbe bought "some licquers & Wines some Flour and some nuts and vegatables." Bryan and Murphy purchased and loaded extra food for the numerous members of their families, though they had some difficulty securing the requisite permits from the customs officers.

The barque put out to sea on April 3, and Valparaiso faded on the horizon. It could still be seen a little before nightfall, looking, according to Abbe, "far more subblime than when we were

[2] John Cody, quoted in the Cleveland *Plain Dealer*, July 16, 1850; MS diary of Eleazer Abbe; and Jones letter of March 19.

close." "But the aspireing Hills and even the lofty Mountains in their rear sunk by degrees until they were lost to our view by the dence fogg." Some of the passengers were sick with bad colds. Dr. Baldwin concluded that George Clute, the Cleveland patternmaker, had "brain fever," but the patient seems to have survived both the disease, whatever it was, and the ministrations of the inexperienced physician.

As the monotonous routine of the voyage resumed, the passengers resorted to the only available and now rather familiar forms of recreation. Shark hunting began immediately. The first shark to be harpooned was such a "huge monster both Harpoons tore out bringing with them a good Part of his entrails." George Harvey then went to work and made a gaff that could be used in landing the great fish. The very next day another shark was harpooned and Harvey brought it aboard with his gaff. All agreed, however, that it was not so big as the one that got away. Harvey and Milo Bennett, the Elyria blacksmith, cut it up for those who cared to partake, and it was "cooked for dinner both by boiling and frying. Some ate of it and some would not ate it but [they] that did ate laugh at them."

Many passed the time playing euchre and chess. Some went in bathing in the warm water when the sea was calm and no sharks were in evidence.

Stacey, the "celebrated Gaimster" from Michigan, got another albatross. George Harvey spent many hours setting the teeth of his saws and sharpening his chisels and planes, so that he would be ready to go to work upon arrival in San Francisco. One day, according to Abbe, "considerable sport was had by some of the passengers ingageing with the sailor men in a regular wheel barrow tumble which gave them an excellent exercise and quite an exciting Laugh or meriment." One evening, when four forty-niners "were having a little civil social dance merely for exercise and not disturbing any one," the captain broke it up in what seemed to Abbe a very "unjenttlemany and abrupt manner."

The whole ship's company was titillated by a juicy little scandal. L. D. Burnell, the supercargo and part owner, took a fancy to Garret Murphy's "amiable" stepdaughter, Maria Malloy, and she seemed to be quite receptive to his attentions. They were seen together constantly and were, of course, the subjects of a good many jesting remarks. One day Llewellyn Rogers, in the presence of Murphy, made some derogatory comments to Ransom Burnell with respect to his brother's relations with this young lady. Murphy implied that Rogers was questioning his stepdaughter's chastity and "rattled off a regular tornado of ill names and threats." No blows seem to have been exchanged, but, as a result of the squabble, parental discipline brought the love affair to an end.

After the *Eureka* was over eight weeks out of Valparaiso and nearing its destination, a row broke out between the other two families: the Bryans and the Skears. Mrs. Skear denounced Mrs. Bryan for "tatling telling and attempting to destroy the carachter of her good name which She Claimed she ever endeaverd to ceep without a blemish." For some reason she blamed her husband also, "calling him a Dastardly coward of a Scoundrel Etc fell uppon him and would probably mellowed his Profile for him had not the passengers interfeared." Undoubtedly these people did get bored with each other's presence in the crowded little after-cabin. It all furnished a little entertainment for the other travelers, including Abbe, who reported it in his diary.

On June 2 he commented: "It is now 2 Months since we have had any sight of Land—t[w]o Months is a long time for Passengers to be cooped up on this dull sailing . . . Bark Eureka." It is a long time on any kind of a ship.

The women were not the only ones who occasionally lost their tempers. Abbe got into a bit of a ruckus himself one day. It seems that he criticized another passenger for "spiting tobacco around and along the front of his berth." According to Abbe's account this "dastardly Tiger of human shape" then sprang upon him while he was "uppon his nees fixing his own Berth." For interfering with an American citizen's sovereign right to spit tobacco juice wherever he wanted to the Elyria farmer got well punched in the head, and suffered some loss of blood from a cut over the "wright" eye.

As the *Eureka* was at sea considerably longer than on either of the preceding legs of the voyage, water and provisions consituted even more of a problem. Within less than three weeks water had become scarce, and passengers were put on a daily allowance of a quart and a half apiece plus a quart and a half to the cooks for each to make tea and coffee and to boil food. Even this rather liberal ration caused some grumbling. Enough water was caught during rains so that no one really suffered for lack of it.

Breakfast sometimes consisted of hard bread soaked in salt water, coffee, cold beef, and pickles. The pickles were considered a great luxury and were supposed to be useful in preventing scurvy. Often the salt beef and pork were bad. After about six weeks the pork was all used up, as were the butter, lard, and molasses. Sugar was running low and the biscuits were made from musty flour.

Various kinds of sea fowl shot and snared by the sportsmen on board made a very welcome supplement to this menu when cooked in stews or pies.　Bird pie parties held in the long boat were important social events.　"I this evening feasted on a bird pie," wrote Abbe on June 11, "by invitation from a party gathered up and partook of it in the long boat which is cald the eating saloon since Bird parties have come fashonable.　The crust was excellent and we enjoyed it quite satisfactorily."

On June 8 they met another Clevelander in mid-Pacific.　David Morris made the trip to California by way of Mexico.　At Mazatlan on the Mexican west coast, he secured passage for San Francisco on a German ship.　The vessel was delayed by calms and contrary winds and eventually ran out of water and provisions.　"Fortunately," Morris wrote to a friend, "a ship came to our relief; you may judge of my joy and surprise to find it the bark *Eureka,* from Cleveland.　The Cleveland boys were all well; they have had a long passage, yet their appearance shows that their 'home on the rolling deep' has been a pleasant one."[3]　So Clevelanders succored a Clevelander on the sea route to California.

Eleazer Abbe recorded the same event in his diary:

A sail was in sight which caused considerable commotion . . . . We ascertained her coullars to be that of hamburgh and they soon hoisted the stars and stripes

　　[3] David Morris to "Dr. Beaumont," San Francisco, June 17, 1850, Cleveland *Plain Dealer,* July 26, 1850.

on the Eureka which was merily cheerd by the Passengers on bord of the Dutch Ship whose passengers
were mostly Americans with a few Mexicans . . . . Her
Capt asked for a cask of water . . . . When we learnt
that they were short of provisions also they took from
the Eureka two bls of hard bread two bls of meal and
one cask of water. We got some interesting news
from them as there passengers had lately come from
the states by the route through Mexico and were
bound for Sanfrancisco.

It was a tedious voyage, the more so because
the experience now lacked novelty. Slowly, oh so
slowly, they climbed the parallels back to the
north. The equator was passed on May 10; there
were no ceremonies. All were shellbacks now,
anyway. "Sailing," wrote the diarist, "is getting to
be an old story with a long tail." There were extended periods of calm when everybody yearned
for the "Exhilarating Darting Spring of the Ship
. . . with the Spirit Stirring onward motion," and
they had plenty of occasion to contemplate "how
useless a thing is a Sail Ship without the wind."

Laboriously they beat up the coast of California. Then on the seventy-sixth day from Valparaiso they swung in through the Gate and
"landed on the long looked for shores of Sanfrancisco full of hope and anxiety for the Gold Mines."

When, on Monday, June 17, 1850, the *Eureka*
let go her anchor in San Francisco Bay, she found
that she had been far outstripped by the *Orion*

and the *Euphrasia,* which had arrived respectively on the sixth and the twenty-sixth of May. On June 18 the San Francisco *Alta California* carried the official announcement of the end of the *Eureka's* voyage: "Barque Eureka, M. Quin [McQueen], 264 days from Cleveland, via Valparaiso 75 days; 59 pass." The *Plain Dealer* published a slightly variant statement from an unidentified exchange: "June 19th—Bark *Eureka,* McQuim, 182 days from Quebec, via Valparaiso, 73 days, 59 passengers, 7 females." In this last notice recognition is appropriately given to the *Eureka's* complement of seagoing Clementines: Mrs. Bryan, the contentious Mrs. Skear, Mrs. Murphy, the three Murphy girls, and the "amiable" Maria Malloy.[4]

William Adair, promoter of the enterprise and co-owner of the vessel, made the journey to California during the winter by way of Panama. On April 1 he wrote to Editor Gray of the *Plain Dealer* from San Francisco. He gave some description of conditions in the city, but naturally could furnish no further information about his ship, which had not left Valparaiso at the time.[5]

As a financial venture the voyage of the *Eureka* was a complete failure. The largest item in its cargo was lumber; the *Alta California* reported on

[4] San Francisco *Alta California,* June 18, 1850; and the *Plain Dealer,* July 25, 1850.
[5] *Plain Dealer,* March 6, May 16, and June 13, 1850.

June 19 that it brought 100,000 feet. Lumber had been in great demand in this rapidly mushrooming community in 1849, and Adair and Burnell had hoped to get four or five hundred dollars per thousand feet for it. But many other ships had come in with cargoes of lumber during the winter and spring, so that by the time the *Eureka* arrived millions of feet were piled up here and there around the waterfront. The price, which had almost dropped through the bottom in the spring, had recovered a bit as a result of the recent fire, but it was still down around sixty to ninety dollars per thousand in late June. Not only were the receipts disappointing, but the obligations incurred at Rio and Valparaiso in raising money to buy supplies had to be met. On July 25, 1850, one creditor secured the issuance of a writ of attachment, sequestering the *Eureka* "together with its tackle, apparel and furniture."[6] Apparently Adair went into bankruptcy. "Adair has busted, blowed up and gone to the devil; so some of the Eureka boys say," wrote a correspondent to the *Plain Dealer* in the fall. "He has made an assignment of his property for the benefit of his creditors, and gone to the mines." As far as our story goes he never came down from the mountains.[7]

[6] This writ of attachment is referred to in the bond signed in connection therewith by the agents of Ventura Sanchez and surety in San Francisco on July 30, 1850, and now in the possession of the California Historical Society.

[7] C. E. Bassett to George G. Washburn, San Francisco, Feb.

Now the Eurekans had their chance to "see the Elephant," and he never seemed to look quite the way he was expected to.

Cyrus Bassett, the former Recorder of Lorain County, wrote of his impressions to George Washburn, editor of the Elyria *Courier.* "I found matters and things quite different than I expected, an exceedingly active, busy as well as large city, . . . much larger than I ever conceived it to be, instead of a small town mostly of shanties and tents it was a city as large as Cleveland nearly." He found the inflated prices very disconcerting and discouraging. "A new comer is taken all aback at the prices which he has to pay . . . ." "To give you a better idea of what a man's dinner might cost him I enclose you a bill of fare of a Restaurant here . . . ; in the bill are forty different articles either one of which costs as much as a good dinner at the Beebe House." The reader gets the impression that Bassett would have been very happy to have had the opportunity to sit down at dinner again in the Beebe House on the square back in Elyria or the Weddell House in Cleveland.[8]

Promptly upon her arrival the *Eureka's* passengers and crew had all gone over the side and struck out into the golden land of California to

28, 1851, Washburn MSS, Western Reserve Historical Society, and letter from "D" in the *Plain Dealer,* Oct. 10, 1850.

[8] Bassett to Washburn, *loc. cit.*

make their fortunes, leaving her, only one of a great fleet of abandoned ships, swinging lonesomely at anchor. A few weeks later the barque *Georgia* from Boston tied up behind her. On board was a Cleveland high school boy, who wrote back to his friends: "The barque Eureka, of Cleveland, lay in shore of us. In my opinion, she will never plough salt water again, having the appearance of being terribly wrenched by the heavy weather of Cape Horn."[9]

In his prophecy of the future of the *Eureka* he was happily wide of the mark. Of that, more later, while we follow the fortunes of a few of its passengers.

[9] Thomas B. Cary, San Francisco, Aug. 17, 1850, in the *Plain Dealer*, Oct. 23, 1850.

9.

Wheel of Fortune

WHEN the Eurekans went ashore they quickly dispersed among the hordes of fortune hunters; they were merged in the flood of emigrants who came from other parts of the United States and from all over the world. Some seem to have become as completely lost to the record of posterity as if they had been dumped into the sea with poor Edward Beardsley, but the names of others reappear in directories, later news items, and elsewhere in the paper middens of the last half of the nineteenth century.

For men who had made a nine months' journey through two oceans in order to get to the land of gold, a surprisingly small number were engaged in gold mining at the end of a year or two. For many the shift to California from Ohio or Michigan or some other part of the East or Middle West brought little change in fortune or even in occupation. It was merely a geographical change for most.

Dr. Baldwin went into the interior for a while; in 1851 he was engaged in mining at Redding Springs in the northern part of the state. While still a comparative newcomer to California he returned to his medical practice. He appears sporadically in the San Francisco directories as a practicing physician from 1859 to 1885, and Mrs. Baldwin is listed as a widow at his former address in 1887. Baldwin was one of the early members of the "Territorial Pioneers of California," and the fact of his having come on the *Eureka* is mentioned in their first annual report.[1]

Andrew Kinninmouth, who had been a blacksmith in Cleveland, became one of the leading citizens of the Georgetown area in California, where he did general blacksmithing, some mining, and a good deal of farming. At one time he owned a large part of the later townsite of Grass Valley

[1] W. A. Grover, *Medical Directory of the Pacific Coast, 1878;* San Francisco directories, 1859, 1862, 1872, 1877, 1882, 1885 and 1887, and Territorial Pioneers of California, *First Annual Report* (San Francisco, 1877), p. 139.

and two considerable ranches in the Bear Creek district. In the seventies and eighties he had a good income from stockraising and the sale of hay and grain. An oldtimer who knew him well described him as "a crusty old Scotchman, but a better man never lived." He was still a bachelor when, in the nineties, he died at the home of a nephew in San Francisco.[2]

William Kewin, after a disappointing experience in the mines and as a carpenter, returned to San Francisco. There he went back to his old occupation as a pattern maker, in which capacity he was associated with the Union Iron Works for a number of years.[3] Llewellyn App Rogers, the Hamilton College graduate, got a job as a schoolteacher in San Francisco. Shortly before the Civil War he returned to his widowed mother, then living in Warren, Pennsylvania, bringing with him approximately six thousand dollars saved from six years' salary as a teacher.[4] Teachers' pay in California seems already to have been somewhat higher than in the East.

Young Henry Lloyd, who had apparently

[2] Letter from Warren T. Russell to Theresa Gay, Oakland, Aug. 19, 1949, and letter to the author, Aug. 15, 1949.

[3] "D.," August, 1850, published in Cleveland *Plain Dealer,* Oct. 10, 1850; San Francisco directories, 1863-1864; 1867-1877, and *Alta California,* Sept. 20, 1870.

[4] Obituary written by L. A. Rogers' brother, published in this paper, the Kane *Republican,* Dec. 8, 1896, and a letter from Secretary Wallace B. Johnson, Hamilton College, Clinton, New York, to the author, Oct. 3, 1952.

worked as a mason and a brewer in Cleveland, secured employment in a brewery in San Francisco, after an abortive trial of mining. A Henry Lloyd, who was killed in a steamboat explosion in 1854, is buried in the old Yerba Buena Cemetery. It is doubtful whether he is the same Henry Lloyd who came on the *Eureka;* if the cemetery records are correct he came from New York.[5] Robert Taylor, it will be recalled, had been a baker in Cleveland. Though the evidence is not available to prove his connections with these establishments, it is to be noted that there were Taylor bakeries in both Sacramento and San Francisco in 1851.[6] Probably the experience of Samuel Grosh as a clerk and retailer in Milan was not wholly irrelevant to his occupation as a partner of Thomas L. Rutherford in the Commercial Flour Mills on First Street in San Francisco, and anybody who had lived in Milan in the forties would have known something about the grain trade.[7]

Schuyler Strong, the Elyria butcher, found gold in an unusual way. It will be recalled that, at the time the search was made for J. S. Benizer's gold pieces, when the *Eureka* was off the coast of Chile, a pair of old boots had been found and auctioned

[5] *Alta California,* April 18, 19, 27, 1854, and burial records of Yerba Buena Cemetery.

[6] Testimony of Alexander Thompson that he worked at Taylor bakeries in Mary F. Williams, *Papers of the San Francisco Committee of Vigilance of 1851* (Berkeley, 1919), III, 301-302.

[7] San Francisco directories, 1863-1864, 1867, and 1877.

off for 62½ cents to this same Schuyler Strong.
Apparently they were pretty good boots (though
rather heavy), because he wore them for a year
before they began to fall apart. One day in the
spring of 1851, when he was in Sacramento, the
tap of one boot became loose. Two gold coins
fell out! He then tore off both soles, finding two
hundred dollars, obviously part of Benizer's lost
hoard. Strong advertised his discovery in a San
Francisco paper. Whether Benizer ever showed
up to retrieve his money is not recorded. Schuyler
Strong must have been an honest man, the kind
of butcher who never leaned on the scales.[8]

A mysterious item in the *Plain Dealer* published in 1851, does not speak so favorably for the
reputation for honesty of another Elyrian. This
other Eurekan is said to have struck it rich very
quickly. According to an anonymous letter, one
of the men from Elyria, not further identified,
"returned from the Southern mines last August
with about $20,000, having been absent just three
weeks." The writer quite clearly meant to imply
that this "strike" had not been made by normal or
legal means.[9]

It is neither unusual nor surprising that a
lawyer in the East should have become a politician
in California. J. Ransom Burnell, the "counsel-

---

[8] Letter from "Deacon," May 1, 1851, *Plain Dealer* June 7,
1851.
[9] *Ibid.*

lor" from Jamestown, New York, and brother of
the shipbuilder and supercargo, was an example.
Before 1860 he is reported to have made fifty thousand dollars raising cattle in the Sacramento valley.
He went into politics, was elected to the state
assembly from Amador County, and was chosen
as speaker of that body in 1861. He became a
state senator in 1862 and president *pro tem* of the
state senate in the following year. He was one of
the organizers of the Union party in California,
formed to support Lincoln and sustain the war.
Later he was an unsuccessful candidate for Congress. In 1876 he was a member of the state Republican committee and of the committee on reso-
lutions at the Republican state convention. The
historian of his county describes him as "a man
of graceful presence, pleasing address, a fluent
speaker, with a good training in the New York
school of politics, of which Martin Van Buren was
the best specimen and *ideal,* whose political gospel
was 'neither give nor take offense.'" It is hard
to tell just how much was supposed to be read
here between the lines.[10]

Some of the cabin boys did pretty well, too.
Young George Hickox, who had irked Dr. Baldwin
by being too forward for his tender age in partici-

[10] J. D. Mason, *History of Amador County, California* (Oakland, 1881) , pp. 94, 100, 102, 105-106, 286; and Winfield J. Davis,
History of Political Conventions in California (Sacramento, 1893),
pp. 205, 363, 612.

pating in debates on board the *Eureka,* became a banker and bullion- and money-broker. Whether he ever dug any gold or not, he handled plenty that others had. In an advertisement in the *Alta California* in 1870 he appears as one of the directors of the "Union Insurance Company of San Francisco."[11]

Apparently Freeman Eggleston must be added to Edward Beardsley and Henry Lloyd as casualties of the *Eureka* adventure. Cholera hit California as well as Ohio. The Sacramento *Courier,* in November of 1850, printed two and a half columns of names of cholera victims in Sacramento and the vicinity. One of these was *"Hinman* Eggleston" of Ohio. There seems to be a better than 50 per cent chance that this is the *Freeman* Eggleston of Independence, Ohio, who had gone out on the *Eureka.* The time elapsed would have given him at least a few months in the Land of Gold.[12]

Some Eurekans actually became miners. Colbert Carthron Huntington, from Painesville, Ohio, was one of those who followed the lure over the mountains to Nevada. In the eighties Huntington was living at Rebel Creek, a small community of cattlemen and miners about forty-five miles north of Winnemuca on the road to Boise, Idaho. In 1886 he was elected mining recorder for that

[11] San Francisco directories, 1863-1864, 1867, and 1877, and *Daily Alta California,* Sept. 20, 1870.
[12] Cleveland *Daily Herald,* Jan. 6, 1851.

area; two years later he was in charge of the registration of voters. One of his nephews remembers how, at about the same time, Huntington revisited Painesville. The youngster was properly thrilled by his visit and his stories of mining life and Indians; the name "Winnemuck" stuck in the boy's mind for over sixty years. The miner brought along a piece of rock with green veins of gold in it, a prime curiosity, which was kept on the parlor table of the Painesville home long after he had returned to Nevada.[13]

The dreams of John Percival Jones, the older of the two Jones boys on the *Eureka,* came true in full and rounded measure. In the early fifties he engaged in mining on the Feather River and in Tuolumne and Calaveras counties with varying success. In 1855 he settled in Trinity County, where he was elected sheriff and then state senator. So, for a time, the California legislature had two Eurekans on its rolls—John P. Jones and Ransom Burnell. Jones ran for lieutenant governor in 1867 but was defeated. Originally a Douglas Democrat, he was associated with Burnell in the early organization of the Union party.

In the year that he was defeated for lieutenant governor, Jones moved to the booming mining

[13] Winnemuca (Nevada) Silver City, Dec. 30, 1886, and July 3, 1888, and Edwin G. Huntington of San Diego, cited by Helen B. Mathews, Painesville, Ohio, in a letter to the author, Feb. 11, 1950.

country in the Washoe district of Nevada, where he became superintendent of the famous Crown Point Mine on the Comstock Lode at Gold Hill. For one reason or another the market value of Crown Point dropped off badly. It was quoted at around a hundred in June of 1868, but in November of 1870 it was hard to get two dollars a share. When everybody else sold, Jones bought. In December of 1870 a rich new ore deposit in the Crown Point mine was uncovered, and by May, 1872, shares of Crown Point stock were selling at $1,000. Almost over night John Jones became one of the richest men in the United States, with an income of over a million dollars a year.[14]

In the very next year Jones was elected by the Nevada legislature to the United States Senate, where he served for thirty years. He was an enthusiastic advocate of free silver (as most silver miners were) and of the protective tariff, an active member of the Senate committee on post offices and post roads, and sponsor of a good deal of mining legislation. For some time after 1876 he devoted a considerable part of his energy to the chairmanship of the United States Monetary Com-

[14] On John P. Jones, see especially the sketch in the *Dictionary of American Biography;* Charles S. Warren, *History of the Santa Monica Bay Region* (Santa Monica, 1934) , pp. 24-31; Hubert Howe Bancroft, *History of Nevada, Colorado, and Wyoming, 1540-1888* (San Francisco, 1890) , p. 149 n. The romanticized version of the voyage of the *Eureka* in Warren seems to have been based upon tradition. See also Davis, *Political Conventions in California,* pp. 111, 205, 235, 249, 267, 363, 634.

mission, which had been established by joint reso-
lution of Congress in that year.   In 1892 President
Harrison sent him to Europe as an American dele-
gate to the International Monetary Conference at
Brussels.   There and elsewhere he was a leading
advocate of international bimetallism.

Senator Jones invested his wealth in a variety
of Western enterprises.   In 1875 he joined with
Senator William M. Stewart and several other
capitalists in the fabulous "mining enterprise at
Panamint, on the west side of Death Valley, . . .
about seventy miles south of Bullfrog, Nevada."
This extremely colorful fragment of the Wild West
was wiped out by a flash flood that swept down
Surprise Canyon and flattened the town in the
summer of 1876.[15]   But this did not make serious
inroads on Jones's vast fortune.   Jones's most important venture, outside of the Comstock, was in
a land development scheme near Los Angeles
which later grew into Santa Monica.

He participated in laying out the Santa Monica
townsite and initiated the construction of a railroad to connect it with Los Angeles.   Though it
was necessary for him as Senator from Nevada to
maintain an official residence at Virginia City, he
probably spent more time in Santa Monica, where
he built his gorgeous mansion, Miramar, in 1888.

[15] William M. Stewart, *Reminiscences* (New York and Washington, 1908), p. 261; and Lucius Beebe, "Panamint, Suburb of
Hell," *American Heritage,* VI (Dec., 1954), 64-69.

His support of the Santa Monica Improvement Company, which laid out a magnificent group of tennis courts, was an important factor in making Santa Monica one of the early centers of interest in tennis in the United States. One of his daughters became women's national champion, and later Santa Monica was the home of such tennis greats as the Sutton sisters, Mary Browne, and Elizabeth Ryan.[16]

Brother Henry Jones did not have a career equaling that of John P., though he was for a while superintendent of the Sumner Mine in Kernville, California. John Jones was married twice but Henry died a bachelor. Another brother, named Thomas after their father, had in the meantime become one of the leading citizens of Cleveland—postmaster, president of the city board of education, president of the city council. In 1891 Thomas, Jr., sent one of his sons to join his wealthy and distinguished uncle in the west.[17]

Several Eurekans left California and returned to the East. "Old Pepper" Howe had returned to Cleveland by March of 1851. The next year he was elected to the city council from the fourth ward.[18] Llewellyn App Rogers returned to the

---

[16] Warren, *History of the Santa Monica Bay Region,* 118-121.
[17] Phelps, *Contemporary Biography of California's Representative Men* . . . , I (San Francisco, 1881), 223-230; and W. Scott Robison, ed., *History of the City of Cleveland* (Cleveland, 1887), appendix, p. xiv.
[18] *Ibid.,* appendix, p. xiii, and *Plain Dealer,* March 15, 1851.

home of his mother in Warren, Pennsylvania. Until his death in 1896 he engaged in "mercantile and lumbering business" in Warren, Tidioute, and other near-by Pennsylvania towns.[19]

Cyrus Bassett, the former county recorder of Elyria, wrote a letter from San Francisco in February, 1851, to his friend George G. Washburn, editor of the Elyria *Courier,* but, significantly, he had nothing to say about his personal activities and prospects. He was back in Elyria by the late fifties, and in 1861 he was soliciting support for re-election as county recorder on the ground that he was "entirely dependent upon" his "daily labor with the pen" for his support. He did not get the job back, but in the seventies secured a federal appointment as deputy collector of internal revenue for Lorain County.[20]

Halsey Doan was forced to work on the streets in San Francisco for a while in order to get capital enough to go to the mines. After a decade as a prospector, he returned to the East in September 1860, still a poor man. Subsequently he was employed for a while as brakeman on the Oil Creek Railway, and later he was a commission merchant in Corry, Pennsylvania. In 1864 he established himself in Cleveland as a dealer in petroleum and

[19] Obituary in Kane *Republican,* Dec. 8, 1896.
[20] Bassett to Washburn, Feb. 28, 1851, Washburn MSS, Western Reserve Historical Society; and Bassett to James Monroe, Elyria, March 9, 1859, June 17, 1861, and May 10, 1872, Monroe MSS in the Oberlin College Library.

a manufacturer of kerosene and gasoline. He is credited with having brought the first tank cars of crude oil to Cleveland from the Pennsylvania oil fields. In partnership with Stephen Harkness, Doan became the chief supplier of petroleum to the Cleveland refineries, and, by 1870, the I. X. L. Oil and Naphtha Works, which he built, was the largest oil refinery in the world. Doan's and Harkness' interests were absorbed in the Standard Oil Company, headed by Doan's friend John D. Rockefeller, who did not waste his time in pursuit of the California gold illusion. So the wealth which escaped Doan in the gold country came to him in the oil business in his home town.[21]

There is no doubt that to W. Halsey Doan belongs the title of "Eurekan who did the most for Cleveland." He rebuilt an abandoned church as Doan's Armory, a structure used not only as a drill hall by the Euclid Light Infantry but as an assembly hall for public lectures, political rallies, and revival meetings. He also later financed the "People's Tabernacle," dedicated to "advancing religion, temperance, and the improvement of the masses." It was in this tabernacle that Moody and Sankey held their five-week Cleveland revival.

When Amasa Stone brought Western Reserve

[21] Ladd, "W. H. Doan," pp. 395-397; William Ganson Rose, *Cleveland, the Making of a City* (Cleveland, c. 1950), pp. 325-326, 526, 533, 539, 543, 556, 563, 573; and, on his friendship with Rockefeller, Nevins, *John D. Rockefeller* I, 257 n., 378.

University to Cleveland from Hudson, he chose Doan to be one of its trustees. Doan joined with Rockefeller and other pious and moralistic Cleveland businessmen in the sponsoring of a campaign for state-wide prohibition in 1883. Finally, in 1885, he donated the land and a considerable part of the money necessary for the erection of the "Music Hall." This hall, which seated between four and five thousand people, was Cleveland's chief public auditorium until it was destroyed by fire in 1898. In it Clevelanders and many from surrounding communities heard Patti and Paderewski, Mark Twain and Henry M. Stanley. Here Charles F. Thwing, president of Western Reserve University, spoke to a mass meeting on the occasion of the four-hundredth anniversary of the discovery of America. Doan died at his Euclid Avenue mansion in 1890.

In midwinter of 1850-1851 Eleazer Abbe, the Elyria diarist, was working by the day for two miner-ranchers at Negro Bar on the South Fork of the American River. A few months later he started home on the ship *Republic,* but it leaked so badly that he and the other passengers had to go ashore on the west coast of Mexico and make their way by other means back to the States. Abbe was reunited with his wife and five children after an absence of about two years. He brought the diary of his outward voyage with him, and it was

in the possession of a granddaughter in Elyria
when the author used it. He lived to be over
ninety.[22]

If this narrative were fictitious, all the questions would be answered. As it is, there are plenty
of loose ends. What became of Adair when he
"blowed up and went to the Devil"? What were
the fates of members of the Bryan, Skear, and
Murphy families? Perchance were Maria Malloy
and L. D. Burnell married when the voyage was
over? Did Orlando Cutter preside at auctions on
Market Street or in Sacramento? Did Benizer ever
get that money back? Perhaps time and some
other investigator will fill some of these gaps.

But enough of the story has been reconstructed
to give an idea of what happened to a sample company of forty-niners, though it is a sample that
was, in all likelihood, somewhat more fortunate
than the general run of prospectors. But it is
meaningless and fruitless to attempt to average the
zero of Beardsley's ocean grave with John P. Jones's
millions and seat in the Senate, or to compare the
satisfactions which came to Huntington from and
his continued search for gold in Nevada with
Jones's finding of it or Llewellyn Rogers' enjoy-

[22] Abbe's MS account of financial relations with Pangborn
and Ely in December, 1850, and January, 1851, at Negro Bar was
found at the back of his MS diary; Nichols and Abbe, *Abbe-
Abbey Genealogy*, p. 159; and *Commemorative Biographical
Record of the Counties of Huron and Lorain, Ohio*, pp. 878-881.

ment of his modest savings and romantic memories back home in Pennsylvania.

The significant generalization is perhaps that all generalizations are compromises with truth and the truest picture of the Gold Rush, or any part of it, must be found at last only in the most complete available sum of the so often contrasting details.

10.

Acapulco

FEW of the ships that carried forty-niners to California ever sailed again. Many were used as boarding houses, warehouses, or saloons; others were torn apart for their lumber; scores of them rotted in the bay where they had been abandoned. Here was the graveyard of the work of many ship carpenters, joiners, and riggers from shipyards all over the world.

But the adventures of the *Eureka* were not over. It was a compliment to her builders that she was one of the few to be chosen to carry passengers again—the triumphant lucky ones with bags of gold, the disappointed who were able to get together enough money to pay their passage back, some recalled to their old homes by reports of illness, death, or financial crisis; some afflicted with just plain homesickness. They thought they had "seen the elephant," and had, very likely, little taste for further adventure as they headed for Massachusetts, Indiana, or Ohio.

In October of 1850, an announcement of the sailing was carried in the columns of the San Francisco *Alta California:*

CALLARD & CO.'S REGULAR LINE FOR REALIJO, PANAMA AND VALPARAISO.—The superior and fast sailing barque EUREKA, E. Coan master, 372 tons burthern, and but three years old, will leave for the above ports on Wednesday, Oct. 23. This barque is fitted for a voyage around Cape Horn, and is undoubtedly prepared for the convenience and comfort of passengers to either of the above ports, on a more extensive scale than any other vessel that has left this season. She has 60 berths and state rooms in the saloon on deck, with a private cabin for families, and a promenade deck 65 feet in length over the same. She will be fitted with beds and bedding entirely new throughout. Her provisions will be of the best the market affords, a list of which may be seen at the office of Callard & Co. Passengers bound for the States will find it to their interest to examine the inducements offered by this vessel before securing tickets elsewhere. For passage only, apply at CALLARD & CO.'S General Passage Office, Clark's Point, from which place the barque may be seen at any time before the day of sailing.[1]

[1] *Alta California,* Oct. 21, 1850.

She was actually cleared on the twenty-sixth of October, three days late,[2] something over four months after she had come in through the foggy Gate after her great voyage from Cleveland. "Old Pepper" Howe, who had complained all the way out about the accommodations, now thought well enough of the *Eureka* to engage return passage on her. If he had only known what was to come!

She sailed away toward the south with a reported 112 passengers, including Howe. Weeks passed and no word was received from her. The weeks lengthened into months. Rumors reached Cleveland that she had been lost with all hands, and then a Mr. Emmons of Buffalo reported that he "saw a man who had conversed with the mate of the *Eureka*," who said that only the mate and two passengers had survived.[3]

In mid-February a circumstantial account of the voyage, based on a report from a passenger, was finally received in Cleveland and published in the *Plain Dealer*. It is brief and to the point and tells the story as well as it is ever likely to be told.

NEWS FROM THE EUREKA

Mr. Griswold, of this city, received a letter yesterday from his brother, who was on board the *Eureka*. It was dated Acapulco, Jan 6th. The vessel left San

[2] "Shipping Intelligence, Port of San Francisco," in *ibid.*, Oct. 27, 1850.

[3] Cleveland *Plain Dealer*, Feb. 3 and 7, 1851.

Francisco in October with 136 passengers for Panama,
had a good sailing breeze for ten days and then was
almost constantly becalmed. After 20 days out, it was
found they were short of water, and the passengers
were put upon short allowance. It soon rained, and
a plentiful supply was caught. After some ten days
more their provisions began to fail, a meeting of the
passengers [was held] and a committee appointed, who
after investigation, reported provisions enough on half
allowance for 15 days only.

After ten days more, no land appearing, another
meeting was called by the committee and rations reduced one third more. The water by this time had
become scarce and ropy, the sea biscuit wormy, and
starvation began to stare the crew in the face; there
was great bitterness and cursing, and some praying.
On the 29th of December land was discovered. Griswold says there was great joy. The pieces of bread,
pork, and other bits of their scanty rations which had
been hid away for a final death struggle with hunger,
was eagerly sought and eat by each passenger. They
were six days after that working the vessel to land,
so perfectly calm was the weather, and during the
time suffered immensely from hunger. The ship had
to be sold or mortgaged to purchase provisions, and
most of the passengers deserted her at Acapulco, al-
though 1500 miles from Panama.[4]

The reports of the United States Consul at
Acapulco verify the story in brief. He recorded
that the barque *Eureka* of 372 tons burthen, Enard
Coan, master, with a crew of 16 and 120 passengers, had arrived from San Francisco on January
5, 1851. Under "General Remarks," he added:

[4] *Ibid.*, Feb. 14, 1851, and more briefly on the same date in
the Cleveland *Daily Herald*.

"Put in here in distress without provisions or water," and "Sold here by the Captain—Fees on discharge of seamen $5.50. Still here."[5]

It has been impossible to explain the inconsistencies in the reports of the number of passengers: 112 cleared from San Francisco, 136 reported unofficially by Griswold and 120 landed at Acapulco. It may be assumed that there were some deaths, but there is nothing to account for an increase. Perhaps the figure 136 represents the total of all persons on board, including the crew.

Acapulco has the finest natural harbor between San Francisco and Panama, a deep, circular bay, surrounded by jungle-clad mountains except for two narrow passages from the sea. Its shores drop so precipitously that, at some places, vessels could tie up directly at the bank, almost under the shadow of the overhanging chaparral. It is one of the hottest places in North America; sometimes for several days in succession the thermometer registers 120° in the afternoon. Still visible is the gash in the encircling hills cut by the Spaniards long ago in an effort to let in a little sea breeze to stir the stifling air.

[5] "Consular Return of the American Vessels arriving at and departing from Acapulco from the 1st day of January to the 30th day of June 1851 inclusive," and "Consular Statement of Fees Received at the United States Consulate at Acapulco from the 1st day of January to the 30th day of June 1851 inclusive," in the General Records of the Department of State, Group No. 59; Consular Despatches, Acapulco, vol. 1, July 18, 1823—December 19, 1853, in the National Archives.

Acapulco had known over two centuries of perennial bustle while it was the eastern port for the Manila galleons. These ships brought each year the silks, spices, jewels, tapestries, rugs, ivory, sandalwood, perfumes, and porcelains of the East to Acapulco's great annual fair. From the fair these exotic luxuries were distributed by pack train and coasting vessels to all Mexico, much of Spanish America, and, indirectly, to Spain itself.

The Manila trade had come to an end in 1815, and Acapulco, never lively except at fair time, had sunk into a steaming decay. Now, in mid-nineteenth century, the town, huddled by the bay, was an unattractive and inconspicuous clutter of stone, wood, and adobe houses, generally not more than a story in height, surrounding a plain little church on the central plaza. Not even the Gold Rush had done much to revive it. Scarcely three thousand permanent residents of varying nationalities took their long siestas on the verandas or in the dim interiors of a few of the dwellings in a community once occupied by at least fifteen thousand.[6]

It is clear that Acapulco was not a very attractive haven for the starving and thirst-crazed passengers and crew who came ashore from the *Eureka.* But it was terra firma, and any land felt

[6] On old Acapulco, see William L. Schurz, *The Manila Galleon* (New York, 1939) ; Bancroft, *California Inter Pocula,* pp. 209-213, and Richard U. Light, "Cruising by Airplane: Narrative of a Journey Around the World," *Geographical Review,* XXV (Oct., 1935), 599-600.

good under foot after the seventy-two days of suffering they had endured in their voyage from San Francisco. After the ship was sold (for a reported $18,000) to finance the rest of their journey, the survivors had to find what accommodations they could on other vessels stopping at Acapulco on their way to Panama. During the remainder of the month, six American vessels cleared from Acapulco for Panama. These were the brig *Leo,* the barque *Trident,* and the steamers *Columbus, Carolina, New Orleans* and *Antelope.* The first to leave after the arrival of the *Eureka* was the *Columbus,* which got away on the twelfth.[7] Any Eurekans who got passage on her had had to wait six days, and many others must have had to stay for weeks. Of course, different passengers had varying luck. One, a Mr. Bottsford of Waukegan, Illinois, was reported back in Buffalo on February 11. "Old Pepper" Howe returned to Cleveland, somewhat less than triumphantly, and without his cane, on March 13.[8]

* * * *

In the summer of 1851 the propeller *Henry Clay* was rebuilt at Black River in Lorain County, Ohio, but business was not so good as it had been a few years before, and no new vessels were launched into the fresh, cool waters of its harbor.

[7] "Consular Return of American Vessels . . . Acapulco."
[8] Cleveland *Daily Herald,* Feb. 17, 1851, and *Plain Dealer,* March 15, 1851.

One Black-River ship, now only four years old but travel-weary, lay abandoned in the bay at Acapulco. The fierce sun bleached the northern pine of her masts and spars, and shrank and cracked her good Ohio oak. Her rotten sails, like the fronds of the palms that fringed the shore, drooped disconsolately in the torpid tropic air.[9] Still legible upon her stern, despite the peeling paint, was the word *Eureka*.

[9] The American consul, as noted above, reported the *Eureka* "still here" on June 1, 1851. There is no later report.

Index

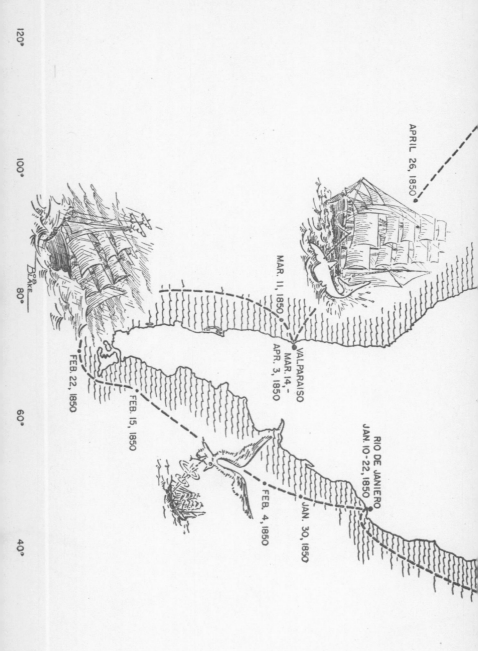

APRIL 26, 1850

MAR. 11, 1850

VALPARAISO
MAR. 14, -
APR. 3, 1850

DRAKE

FEB. 22, 1850

FEB. 15, 1850

FEB. 4, 1850

RIO DE JANIERO
JAN. 10-22, 1850

JAN. 30, 1850

20°

40°

120°

100°

80°

60°

40°